ALL YOU NEED TO KNOW ABOUT THE BIBLE

C000001836

Book 4:
a journey from then to now

BRIAN H EDWARDS

DayOne

© Day One Publications 2017

ISBN 978-1-84625-587-8

All Scripture quotations, unless stated otherwise, are from The Holy Bible, New International Version Copyright © 1973, 1978, 1984 International Bible Society

British Library Cataloguing in Publication Data available

Published by Day One Publications
Ryelands Road, Leominster, HR6 8NZ
Telephone 01568 613 740   Fax 01568 611 473
North America Toll Free 888 329 6630
email—sales@dayone.co.uk
web site—www.dayone.co.uk

All rights reserved
No part of this publication may be reproduced, or stored in a retrieval system, or transmitted, in any form or by any means, mechanical, electronic, photocopying, recording or otherwise, without the prior permission of Day One Publications.

Cover design by Kathryn Chedgzoy
Printed by T J International

ALL YOU NEED TO KNOW ABOUT THE BIBLE

BRIAN H EDWARDS

Book 4
A journey
from then to now

The series outline

Book 1 Can we trust it?
What this book is all about

1. **What's the Bible all about?**
   The Master Plan with Jesus Christ as the theme

2. **Remarkable prophecy**
   What do we do with these incredible predictions?

3. **Evidence of an eyewitness**
   Proof that the writers were there

4. **Did Jesus really live?**
   Jesus fixed in history

5. **Living letters for living churches**
   Marks of real letters to real Christians

6. **Fact or fiction?**
   Evidence of the Old Testament written in its time

Book 2 Big claims from a unique book

1. **The God who reveals himself**
   Evidence everywhere

2. **Ultimate truth**
   God-given and without error

3. **Jesus and his Bible**
   What Scriptures did Jesus use?

4. **The apostles and their Bible**
   What Scriptures did the apostles use?

5. **Absolute authority**
   Big claims by prophets, Jesus, and apostles

6. **Is the Bible enough?**
   Sufficient and final

7. **The Chicago statement**
   The inerrancy statement of the International Council for Biblical Inerrancy

Book 3 Have we got the right books?

Book 4 A journey from then to now

Book 5 Sense as well as faith

1. Tearing the Bible apart
The Bible and its critics

2. Great minds on a great book
What scholars say

3. Digging up the evidence
Archaeology confirms the truth

4. Guidelines for combat
Errors and contradictions?

5. Solving the problems
Resolving some of the issues

Book 6 Enjoy your Bible!

1. It's for you, it's alive—read it!
The best way to read the Bible

2. Reading the Bible with common sense
A guide to a good understanding

3. A bit more common sense
Types, symbols and dangers to avoid

4. Getting to grips with the Old Testament
A chart of the books in their proper place

5. Piecing the Gospels together
A harmony of the life of Jesus

6. Where did they write their letters?
The Acts of the Apostles and where all the letters fit in

7. Reading the Bible from cover to cover
A careful plan to read it all in eighteen months!

8. Take time with God
Spending time each day with God

Contents

What this book is all about

Each year thousands of books, articles and magazines with the Bible as their subject pour into the bookshops and libraries and onto the tablets, iPads and smart phones of the world, and movies make money when they make the Bible their theme. More copies of the complete Bible are printed and distributed each year in over five hundred and fifty languages (and rising annually), than any other book.

The Bible moulded the English language as we know it. Shakespeare was familiar with the translation known as the *Geneva Bible* and he allowed it to shape his use of the language. Every day, English speaking people across the world are using words, phrases and expressions that are straight from the Bible—though they are mostly quite unaware of this: 'feet of clay', 'tell it not in Gath', 'iron sharpens iron', 'a drop in a bucket', 'for such a time as this', 'faithful are the wounds of a friend', 'a wolf in sheep's' clothing', 'an angel of light', 'escaping by the skin of my teeth', 'how the mighty are fallen', 'put not your trust in princes', 'killing the fatted calf', 'our days are numbered', 'the writing on the wall', 'filthy lucre' and 'eat, drink and be merry, for tomorrow we die'.

Words like 'shibboleth', 'scapegoat', 'Exodus' and 'Promised Land' have slipped into our language straight from the Bible. Even Bible characters are more quoted than known: 'Adam's apple', 'Samson's strength', 'Job's comforters', 'David and Goliath', 'the wisdom of Solomon', 'Daniel in the lions' den', 'doubting Thomas', and 'a Judas'.

The Bible stands alone among books not only because of its clarity, longevity and popularity, but because of the opposition it has attracted to itself. Throughout its history, even while it was being written, its enemies have tried to destroy it. It has been burned, banned and its readers have been imprisoned and murdered for reading it—and across large areas of the world they still are.

This fourth book in the series, begins by tracing the story of how a few attempts had been made to translate parts of the Bible into the English language before, late in the fourteenth century, John Wycliffe and his team translated the whole Bible from the Latin *Vulgate*. Every book of this translation from a translation had to be copied by hand. The early evangelicals bravely carried Wycliffe's Bibles with them as they preached across the land; many died for their courage, but the fire of the Reformation had been lit.

By 1526 printing had reached Europe and William Tyndale presented the world with its first New Testament printed in English and translated from the original Greek. The Reformation in England now had God's written authority for its gospel of justification by faith alone, in a language that even the ploughboy could understand. Ten years later Henry VIII ordered every church to display a copy of the complete Bible in English—but it had tragically cost many lives. Book four surveys some of the most significant translations up to, and including, the *King James Authorized Version* in 1611.

Turning the clock back, chapters 2 and 3 pause to ask how old are the earliest Hebrew and Greek copies of our Old and New Testaments? What are the various manuscripts of the Hebrew and Greek available today for constructing the biblical text? And how much do we know about the care with which copies of the Bible were made? Unlike almost all other surviving texts of ancient literature, the Bible has a rich and valuable storehouse of copies that contribute to establishing an accurate text for translation. The amount of material available may be a surprise to many readers. Even more so, the overwhelming agreement between one manuscript and another, and the evidence that the New Testament books were circulating before the end of the first century.

However, in some parts of the Bible there is conflicting evidence between one ancient manuscript and another. It is rare in the Old Testament but more frequent in the New. But, as one New Testament scholar expressed it: 'not one thousandth part' is affected in this way. In chapter 4, 'Discovering the best text', some of these issues are explained and illustrated. No one needs to be intimidated by what is known as 'textual criticism'. The integrity of the Bible is enhanced, not diminished, by the vast amount of material available and the overwhelming areas of complete agreement where not a single manuscript is in disagreement.

The concluding chapter takes up the story of Bible translations from the *King James Authorized Version* onwards. The plethora of Bible translations and paraphrases today is bewildering and we need to be sure what we are looking for in a good translation.

Whatever translation is chosen, those who know their Bibles are aware of some of the criticisms that have been levelled against its authority and accuracy. In the next book, the reader can stand with some of the greatest scholars of the biblical and archaeological world and declare that 'Christianity did not originate in a lie, and we can and must demonstrate this.'

1. From flames to fame

The Bible is the most translated book in the world. More than one third of the world's six thousand languages—and that covers ninety percent of the world's population—have all or part of the Bible.

Millions of copies of the English Bible are printed and sold each year. But this is not a modern phenomenon: in the sixteenth century, during the reign of Elizabeth I when the population of Britain was less than six million, around half a million copies of the Bible were printed; this figure doubled by the time of the Commonwealth under Cromwell and the Puritans.

As the Christian gospel spread across the Roman world, so the Bible spread with it. Two years before his death in AD 384, Pope Damascus had instructed his secretary and able scholar Eusebius Sophronius Hieronymus (Jerome) to provide the church with a definitive translation of the Bible. It would be in Latin, which was the official language of both church and state across Western Europe.

Jerome had learnt Hebrew earlier in his life, and although he began by revising the Old Latin texts of the Old Testament, by AD 405 he had completed the Old Testament from the Hebrew into Latin. All previous Latin versions of the Old Testament had been made from the *Septuagint*, the Greek translation of the Hebrew Scriptures. He used only the books from the Jewish collection which meant that he did not include any from the *Apocrypha*; he was later compelled to add the *Apocrypha*, and he simply copied these from the Old Latin and made it clear that these were church books and not canonical books.

For the New Testament, Jerome knew that there were many poorly copied and corrupted texts in Latin and he made the obvious decision to translate from the original Greek. In the event, his translation of New Testament books was limited to the four Gospels and the remainder he appears to have taken from Old Latin texts.[1] However, his own translations were excellent and in a Latin that people could understand, hence it was known as the *Vulgate*, meaning 'the common tongue'. Despite the often fierce opposition to Jerome's new translation, in 1546 the Roman Catholic Council of Trent, declared that the *Vulgate* was the only authorized text for the Bible and an anathema was placed on all who disagreed. For centuries following, the Latin *Vulgate*, including the selected books from the *Apocrypha*, was accepted uncritically.

The Anglo-Saxons and their Bible

In AD 43, during the reign of the emperor Claudius, the Romans arrived in what became Britannia Romana. Christianity almost certainly arrived very soon after, if not before. The twelfth century legend of Joseph of Arimathea, and even the apostle Peter, visiting Britain have little history to support them. However, what we do know is that Pomponia Graecina, the wife of General Plautius who led the victorious Roman army into Britain for the emperor, was later charged with adopting a 'foreign superstition', at that time a certain reference to Christianity.[2] She had been in Britain with her husband. We also know that Caratacus, the British chieftain and his family were captured on the Welsh border and taken to Rome where Claudius spared his life; he would have been in Rome at the same time as the apostle Paul. The suggestion that he and his family were baptised by Paul lacks historical evidence.[3]

How early the first texts of Scripture could have arrived on the shores of Roman Britain will depend upon our view of the dating of the Gospels; the evangelistic passion of the early church and the rapid spread across Asia recorded in the Acts of the Apostles, leaves little doubt that Christians carried the gospel wherever they travelled. Alban, the first known Christian

---

1 F F Bruce, *The Canon of Scripture* (IVP Academic, Illinois, 1988), pp. 87–93.
2 Tacitus refers to her trial in Annals XIII. 32.
3 For an interesting discussion on the possibility of the family of Caratacus being committed into the care of Pomponia and a reference to her and her son in Romans 16:13 and her son in 2 Timothy 4:21, see 'The Early Writing of the Gospel' by W R Cooper in *The Tyndale Society Journal* (Oxford, No. 37, Autumn 2009), pp. 32–39.

martyr in Britain, was put to death in Verulamium (St Albans) in the early or late third century. Gildas, writing in Britain in the fifth or sixth century, claims that the gospel arrived 'as we know, in the last years of Tiberius Caesar.'[4] Whether or not Gildas is correct, it is certain that before AD 222 Tertullian, the bishop of Carthage in North Africa, could boast that 'parts of Britain inaccessible to the Romans were indeed conquered by Christ.'[5] In August 314, five representatives (including three bishops) of the church in Britain attended the Council of Arles.

However, when the Romans left Britain before the end of the fourth century, Christianity declined. The invasions from Angles, Saxons and Jutes across the channel, meant that the Anglo-Saxons brought their pagan religions with them. When Augustine arrived on the shores of Kent in AD 597 there was, apparently, little evidence of the gospel.

Even when the first Scriptures arrived, a text in Old Latin was of little use to the Anglo-Saxons apart from the few educated clerics. Gildas quoted Scripture, so he must have had some portions of the Bible. For many centuries, the way in which Bible stories were communicated to the ordinary people was through the preaching of travelling friars, the mediaeval miracle plays and the decoration of churches by wall paintings, carvings and later by stained-glass windows. The Latin liturgy of church services was unintelligible to most, but the elaborate ceremonies and ornate dress of the priests were all intended to instruct the people. The people also learnt poems and songs which they used at their gatherings. One of the most gifted poets was a labourer called Caedmon, who eventually joined the monastery at Whitby in East Yorkshire because of his gift of turning Bible stories into simple poems and songs for the people.[6]

---

4 Tiberius reigned AD 14-37. Gildas, *De Excidio et Conquestu Britanniae* (The Overthrow and Conquest of Britain). A sermon against the corruption of the kings and church in Britain. His history is not always reliable, but he writes as if his readers will know how early the gospel came to Britain.

5 Tertullian, *An Answer to the Jews*, VII.4, trans. S Thelwall.

6 For more on Caedmon see David Daniell, *The Bible in English* (Yale University Press, New Haven and London, 2003), pp. 39–41. Daniell's scholarly book provides an excellent resource for this subject of the Bible in English.

The language which was spoken by the Anglo-Saxon people of Britain before the Norman conquest of 1066 is known as Old English. It was so different from our modern English that it is virtually another language. A poem recounting the story of the Exodus from Egypt closes with the words: 'It is the eternal God of Abraham, creation's Lord, who this camp protects, valiant and powerful with a mighty hand.' In the Old English it appears as: 'This is se ecea Abrahames god, frumsceafta frea, se thas fyrd wereth modig and maegenrof mif thaere miclan hand.'

At first there was little obvious reason to translate the Bible into English. The common people could not read and the priests were supposed to be able to understand their Latin Bible. For this reason, the existing books, some beautifully decorated, are texts either in Old Latin or the *Vulgate* of Jerome.

It is believed that Aldhelm, the first Bishop of Sherborne in Dorset, was the first to begin some translation about the year AD 700; he commenced with the Psalms. Bede, a monk at Jarrow, around AD 731 wrote the first *History of the English Church and People*. Bede reveals a wide knowledge of the Bible and apparently translated parts of the New Testament; he began a translation of John's Gospel 'into our mother tongue, to the great profit of the Church.' It is likely that he translated more, but unfortunately none of his translation work has survived. He urged that the less able priests should be taught the *Apostles' Creed* and the Lord's Prayer in English. Seven hundred years later men, women and children were burnt at the stake in England for taking his advice.

By the mid-ninth century the Vikings, who traded—though mostly raided—across the North Sea, were causing havoc in East Anglia and further inland. Alfred the Great, king of Wessex from 871 until his death in 899, should be remembered not only for burning cakes, building a navy and beating the Danes—although by doing so he rescued the English language from becoming Old Norse. He was a just and educated king whose Christian faith was real. How much translation Alfred undertook himself, and how much his scholars accomplished on his behalf, is uncertain. In addition to many good books ('most needful for men to know') into English, under Alfred's rule the Ten Commandments (which headed Alfred's law code) and other parts of Exodus and Acts were translated. Before his death more than fifty biblical Psalms could be read by the Anglo-Saxon people in their own tongue. The significance of this is that at this time, there was almost no known translation of the Scriptures in any common language across Europe. The single exception being a Gothic translation (known as *Codex Argenteus*) by Ulfilas around AD 350.

The *Wessex Gospels* are the first example we possess of a translation of the Gospels into Old English, and they are dated sometime after the death of Alfred in the tenth century. Later in that century Aelfric, a scholarly abbot at Eynsham in Oxfordshire, made a translation of the first seven books of the Old Testament (his *Heptateuch*). Whilst the Latin translation continued to circulate, sometimes a helpful monk would add an English translation to it. The *Lindisfarne Gospels*, exquisitely and colourfully decorated and now in the British Library, is perhaps the most famous example of this. It was originally copied towards the end of the seventh century, and two hundred and fifty years later an obliging priest named Aldred added a literal English translation in the Northumbrian dialect between the lines.

The Norman Conquest—a blow to the Bible

The conquest by William of Normandy changed not only the nature of the church in England, but the English language and culture. The new lords were Norman-French, and within a short time the old Wessex Gospels would have been virtually unintelligible even to the ordinary people. The evolution of the English language from the Norman conquest is a fascinating subject that partially explains why English is such a rich and full language today.[7] Anglo-Saxon and Norman-French muddled along together, compounded by scattered dialects which meant that the inhabitants of one area close to another often spoke mutually incomprehensible languages. Slowly a new language—a mixture of many strands—emerged; it is known to us as Middle-English.

---

7 For the story of the English language see Melvyn Bragg, *The Adventure of English* (Hodder and Stoughton, London 2003).

However, whilst the language of law and church remained Latin, communication for the court and nobles was Norman-French. Translations of parts of the Bible into an anglicized French were of little value and, with the ever-increasing authority of the pope as the absentee landlord at Rome, Bible translation took a step backwards. Until the middle of the fourteenth century it apparently never occurred to anyone that a whole Bible in the language of the people might be a good thing. Occasionally parts of the Bible were translated by individuals, and Richard Rolle, the godly hermit of Hampole near Doncaster, translated the Psalms into prose early in the fourteenth century. But such translations were chiefly for the benefit of the priests, monks and nuns, and all were from the Latin *Vulgate* of Jerome.

Without the Bible in the vernacular, the masses were treated to legend and romance to such an extent that William Tyndale later complained that the illiterate masses knew more about Robin Hood than about the Bible. Often legend and Bible stories were so interwoven that the ignorance of the people was compounded. An Anglo-Norman translation of the book of Revelation was produced, and appears to have been popular, but apparently little more in English. For three hundred years, the story of the Bible in English came to a tragic full stop.

John Wycliffe—the first Bible in English

At the beginning of the thirteenth century King John of England was tired of Pope Innocent III, and the feeling was mutual. To bring the king in line, the pope ordered the church to take industrial action by refusing all marriages, baptisms and burials. Bowing to this pressure, King John signed away his crown and kingdom to the pope, and the knights responded by forcing the king to sign the Magna Carta in 1215, a people's charter of rights. The knights and barons were determined not to let either king or pope have unrestricted power in England.

John Wycliffe was born in 1324 near Richmond in Yorkshire into a nation of misery, intrigue and religious abuse. Two decades later, two rival popes vied for power, and the plague killed a third of the population of Europe—two hundred a day were dying in London alone. Not surprisingly Wycliffe's first tract, in 1356, was called *The Last Age of the Church*. Four years later, when Master at Balliol College, Oxford, he began his attack against the wandering friars who robbed and deceived the people. Wycliffe also defended the right of the king to rule in England. This theologian from Oxford—he held the chair of Divinity from 1372—was popular among the nobility, and even the powerful John of Gaunt, Duke of Lancaster, became his patron.

In his writings, Wycliffe frequently quoted from Scripture and evidently he had access to a Latin Bible. He wrote against the abuses and errors of Rome and survived every attempt to silence him. Summarising the nation, he concluded, 'The chief cause, beyond doubt, of the existing state of things, is our lack of faith in Holy Scripture … It is His [God's] pleasure that the books of the Old and New Law should be read and studied.' For this, the people must have the Bible in English. There had been scattered attempts to translate parts of the Bible, and by the time of Wycliffe there were at least three versions of the Psalms in Middle-English, including a prose version by the hermit Richard Rolle. Parts of the Gospels and the Apocalypse of John had also been translated.

Wycliffe and his team set out their threefold purpose in translating the Bible: first, to test and correct the doctrine of the church; second, to anchor men's experiences in the truth; and third, to lead men and women to Christ. Aided by Nicholas of Hereford and others, Wycliffe completed the translation of the Bible from the Latin *Vulgate* well before his death in 1384. Following this, there were many new editions and John Purvey was responsible for the most enduring of them all in 1388.

Here is Hebrews 1:1–4 in Wycliffe's translation:

'Manyfold and many maners sum tyme God spekinge to fadris in prophetis, at the laste in thes daies spak to us in the sone: whom he ordeynede eyr of alle thingis, by whom he made and the worldis. The which whanne he is the schynynge of glorie and figure of his substaunce, and berynge alle thingis bi word of his vertu, makyng purgacioun of synnes, sittith on the righthalf of mageste in high thingis; so moche maad betere than aungelis, by how moche he hath inherited a more different name bifore hem.'

This first edition was a fairly literal translation from the Latin *Vulgate*, and therefore a translation from a translation. Subsequent revisions showed greater concern to be read easily and reflect English idioms. Many copies of the *Vulgate* included the spurious Epistle to the Laodiceans (see Book 3 chapter 8 in this series); Wycliffe faithfully translated it, placed it after Colossians and noted: 'But this epistle is not in common Latin books, and therefore it was but late translated into English tongue.'

Many who were influenced by the writings of John Wycliffe went out as 'Poor Preachers' throughout England and Wales, each with a copy of the Bible in his hand. They were mockingly referred to as 'Lollards'—a word that probably meant something like 'mumblers'. For the first time in thirteen centuries the Englishman had the whole Bible in his own tongue. Without the printing press, every copy was handwritten; astonishingly, some twenty copies of the complete Bible and around ninety of the New Testament (which compares well with the extant sixty-four copies of Chaucer's *Canterbury Tales*) have survived to this day. This is surprising when we consider the strong opposition that it was met with by the authorities.

Whilst, to a modern reader, parts of the Wycliffe Bible may be hard going, in its day it was in the language of ordinary people—rough and common. The Bible came alive to them, just as Tyndale's would a century and a half later, and that was the intention of Wycliffe and his team. The translations that the courageous Lollards carried with them across the country also opened the door to commentaries on the Bible; people could now discuss the Bible because they knew what it said. At last they could read for themselves in Ephesians (2:8–9) 'For by grace ye ben sauyd bi feith, and this is not of you; for it is the yifte of God. Not of werkis, that no man haue glorie'—and that presented a gospel completely at variance with the teaching of Rome.

The church responded in alarm. In 1394 a bill was presented to Parliament forbidding anyone to read the Bible in English without a bishop's licence. 'What!' exploded John of Gaunt in 1390 when the House of Lords was presented with a motion to burn all Wycliffe's Bibles, 'Are we the very dregs of humanity that we cannot possess the laws of our religion in our own tongue?' Nearly two decades after Wycliffe's death, the Archbishop of Canterbury wrote to the pope about 'This pestilent and wretched John Wyclif, of cursed memory, that son of the old serpent...' The Bible in the mother tongue was scattering 'pearls before swine', and it was the firm belief of the learned divines of the day that the Bible was given, not to the people, but to the church to interpret for the people. A few scattered attempts at translation over the centuries was one thing, but a whole Bible in English was quite another.

Between 1401 and 1409 the church took vigorous steps to ensure that it could hand over to the state for public burning those convicted of heresy— and translating or reading a Bible in English was heresy. Archbishop Thomas Arundel's *Constitutions against the Lollards* of 1408 forbade anyone to own even a text from the English Bible without a bishop's licence, and the penalty for disobedience was often death.

The actual wording of the prohibition drawn up in Oxford in 1408 forbad the translation of 'any text of Holy Scripture into the English or any other language, by way of a book, pamphlet, or tract' and that no such translation could be read 'in part or in whole, publicly or privately' until the translation was approved by the church authorities. However, the authorities had no intention of allowing the public at large to read the Holy Scripture in English. The Latin *Vulgate* was the only permitted text.

Paragraph 7 included:

'The translation of the text of Holy Scripture out of one tongue into another is a dangerous thing ... therefore we enact and ordain that no one henceforth do by his own authority translate any text of Holy Scripture into the English tongue or any other by way of book, pamphlet, or treatise. Nor let any such book, pamphlet, or treatise now lately composed in the time of John Wicklif or since, or hereafter to be composed, be read in whole or in part, in public or in private, under pain of the greater excommunication, till that translation have been approved by the diocesan of the place, or if occasion shall require, by a provincial Council. Let him that do contrary be punished in the same manner as a supporter of heresy and error.'[8]

---

8   The text (in Latin) of the Constitution adopted by Archbishop Thomas Arundel and the Provincial Council at Oxford 1408, recorded from Lyndewode's *Provinciale*, Antwerp, Christopher of Endhoven, December 20, 1525. In David Wilkin's *Concilia Magnae Britanniae et Hiberniae* (London 1737), Vol. III, p. 317.

England was exceptional across Europe in its violent and cruel opposition to the vernacular Bible. These *Constitutions of Oxford* were applied so vigorously that by the early sixteenth century Wycliffe's Bible was scarce. However, the effect of the Bible was to bring both revival and reformation into the nation, and the later revisions of Wycliffe's Bible enjoyed great popularity throughout the fifteenth century. One hundred and fifty years after the death of Wycliffe, Sir Thomas More, the ill-fated Chancellor to Henry VIII, was grumbling that you could not meet two men on the roads of England 'without one of them being a Wycliffite.'

The *General Prologue*, to Wycliffe's Bible, published around 1395, set out the principles of translation which Wycliffe and his team had adopted. The first need was to find the best Latin text and then to understand it:

'First of all this simple creature went to much trouble, with various friends and helpers, to gather many old bibles, and other books written by theologians, and commentaries, in order to edit one Latin bible somewhat correctly; and then he studied the text and whatever commentaries he could get, especially the commentaries of Nicolas of Lyra on the old testament, which was very helpful in this work; then he referred to the old grammarians and theologians for the interpretation of difficult words and passages, to see how they might best be understood and translated; and then he translated as clearly as he could the meaning, and in this task he also was helped by many good and knowledgeable friends, who suggested corrections to the translation.'

Then follows the method of translating:

'It should be known that the best way of translating out of Latin into English is to translate according to the meaning, and not merely according to the words, so that the meaning might be as plain, or even more plain, in English as in Latin, while not straying any further from the literal translation than is necessary. The letter need not always be closely followed in the translation, but by all means let the meaning be completely plain, for the words of a translation should serve to convey the intended meaning, or else the words are useless or false … and I ask, for the sake of love and the common benefit of Christian souls, that if any learned man find any fault in the translation, let him substitute a better interpretation of the Latin himself. But he should first of all see to it that his Latin text is correct, for he will find that many of the Latin copies are often incorrect if he examine many of them, especially the newer ones.'

Finally, the life of the translator himself came under scrutiny:

'...and he must also live a clean life, and be very devout in his prayers, and not have his mind distracted by worldly things, so that the Holy Spirit, who is the author of all wisdom and knowledge and truth, will prepare him in his work, and prevent him from making mistakes ... By this manner, with good living and great labour, men may come to a true and clear translating and understanding of the scriptures, however hard it may seem at the beginning. May God grant to us all the grace to know well and fully obey the holy scriptures, and suffer joyfully some pain for it in the end! Amen.'[9]

Despite being excommunicated by the pope, Wycliffe was supported by many people of influence, including John of Gaunt, Lord Cobham, the Earl of Shaftesbury, the Queen Mother, and Anne of Bohemia—the wife of Richard II; at her death in 1391 Anne possessed the four Gospels in English. Wycliffe 'retired' to the parish of Lutterworth in Leicestershire where he died on Christmas Day 1384.

William Tyndale—the first printed Bible

Constantinople fell to the Islamic forces in 1453, William Caxton set up his printing press close by Westminster Abbey in 1476, and the Dutch theologian Desiderius Erasmus arrived in Cambridge in 1511. These three events were each equally significant in the development of the English Bible. Scholars fled to the west from the ancient capital of the Christian Byzantine empire with priceless manuscripts of the Greek New Testament; by 1516 Erasmus was ready to publish the Greek New Testament in Germany, and printing presses were at hand to spread rapidly the influence of the Bible. However, it was James Nicholson, a printer in Southwark, who had the honour of being the first to print a Bible in England—*Coverdale's Bible*. The first paper-mill was established in England in 1490, a century after Wycliffe's Bible was painstakingly copied and recopied by hand and, by a neat coincidence, within a year or two of the birth of William Tyndale.

---

9 A modern English version of chapter 15 of John Purvey's *Prologue to the Wyclif Bible*, translated from the Middle English text by Terence P Noble. On line.

England was well behind the continent both in printing and in the acceptance of a vernacular Bible. There were more than a thousand printers established on the continent of Europe whilst only three, including Caxton, resided in England where the authorities were relentlessly opposed to the English Bible. Germany had its first translation in 1466, France in 1474, Italy in 1471, Bohemia in 1474, Holland in 1477, and even Spain before the turn of the century. All these were from the Latin. Luther's New Testament translated from the Greek came in 1522. England was the most conservative and Catholic of all the pope's estates.

Tyndale, a graduate of Oxford, trained for the priesthood, came to a living faith in Christ, and early decided to give the Englishman a translation he could easily read. He studied the Greek texts of Erasmus, and when Tyndale arrived at Little Sodbury Manor in Gloucestershire in 1521 to tutor the two children of Sir John and Lady Walsh, he was already preparing the first drafts of his New Testament translation. It was here, in debate with a priest who was visiting the manor and who maintained 'we would be better without God's laws than the pope's', that Tyndale declared his life's ambition: 'I defy the pope and all his laws; if God spare my life, ere many years I will cause a boy that driveth a plough shall know more of the Scripture than thou dost.' He had been reading Erasmus, who had already made the same comment in a preface to the Greek New Testament.

Since there was no place in England for a Bible-translating priest, Tyndale slipped across to the continent, and in 1525 his New Testament was coming off the press of Peter Quentel in Cologne. The work was discovered after a few sheets had been printed and Tyndale and his colleague fled to Worms where, after a hasty revision of the text, the New Testament was printed in 1526 and copies of the contraband book landed in England the same year, smuggled in by the German merchants whose warehouse was on the bank of the Thames in London.[10]

---

10 For the life of Tyndale and his translations see Brian Edwards, *William Tyndale – England's greatest Bible translator* (Day One Publications, Leominster, England 2009).

From the merchants and carriers, the books were passed to the couriers across England. At All Hallows, Honey Lane in London, Robert Forman was busy with the illicit trade and, together with his curate Thomas Garrett, by February 1526 they had moved 350 Bibles and Lutheran books to Oxford before Garrett's arrest. Barrels, boxes and packets were marked to identify the books and, although Thomas More occasionally broke a prisoner under torture and learned the marks, much of the contraband got through.

One of the most successful 'book smugglers' was Richard Bayfield. Ordained a priest in 1518 he first met with the true gospel when two bricklayers gave him Tyndale's New Testament along with two other books of Tyndale. He was arrested, whipped and placed in the stocks. Later, he joined Tyndale in Antwerp and made many journeys carrying books from the continent, until he was betrayed and taken to the infamous Lollards Tower in Lambeth Palace. Here he was forced to stand against a wall and chained at the neck, waist and legs—but he refused to betray his contacts. He freely admitted that over a period of eighteen months he had brought 'a great number of [books of] every sort' into the country. He was condemned and burnt at Smithfield on Monday 20 November 1531.

As with the Wycliffe Bible, the bishops hated this New Testament. Tunstall of London ordered it to be burnt and wrote to his archdeacons on 24 October 1526 complaining of the 'holy gospel of God' in the common tongue which was intermingled with 'certain articles of heretical depravity and pernicious erroneous opinions, pestilent, scandalous, and seductive of simple minds … of which translation many books, containing the pestilent and pernicious poison in the vulgar [common] tongue, have been dispersed in great numbers throughout our diocese; which truly, unless it be speedily foreseen will without doubt infect and contaminate the flock committed to us, with the pestilent poison and the deadly disease of heretical depravity.' [11] At which point the bishop seems to have exhausted his store of expletives.

---

11 See above, p. 78.

Such language was calculated to make the laziest archdeacon wake up and act. Within thirty days, all copies must be handed in, upon pain of excommunication and the charge of heresy. The following day the bishop marshalled the London booksellers before him in a private chapel and warned them of the consequences of handling 'Lutheran books', whether in Latin or English.

Not only were the booksellers and traders warned, but severe punishment was handed out to those who were discovered with a New Testament in their possession. However, a New Testament, translated from the original Greek and printed so that it could be reproduced in quantity and with speed, was a gift that Englishmen would not turn down. Copies rapidly spread across the country and even the students at Cardinal Wolsey's new college at Oxford were avidly reading it. Labourers would barter a load of hay for a copy.

Tyndale was well qualified to translate. According to Hermannus Buschius, the Renaissance Humanist who had lectured in literature and rhetoric at Cologne prior to Tyndale's arrival, in addition to his native English, William Tyndale was proficient in Latin, Italian, Spanish, French, German, Greek and Hebrew. Buschius added that, 'whichever he speaks, you would think it his native tongue.' Bishop Westcott, the nineteenth century New Testament scholar, commented, 'He deals with the text as one who passed a scholar's judgement upon every fragment of the work, unbiased by any predecessor.' Among the list of helps that the translator tells us he possessed, he had read the German translation by Martin Luther that arrived in England in September 1522. Although it served the purpose of the churchmen to dub Tyndale 'Lutheran', in fact he was quite independent of the German Reformer in his translation. Oddly, he never refers to Wycliffe's translation, and in his preface to the reader he claimed that he had no one to copy and none to help him with the English 'or eny that had interpreted [translated] the same or soche lyke thige [thing] in the scripture before tyme.' This preface 'To the Reder' in his New Testament reveals his gospel heart:

'Give diligence dear Reder (I exhorte the) that thou come with a pure mynde and as the Scripture sayth with a syngle eye unto the wordes of health and of eternal lyfe: by the which (if we repent and beleve them) we are borne a newe created a fresshe and enjoye the frutes off the bloud of Christ.' Tyndale urged his readers to notice the plain and clear parts of Scripture and to be careful in hard places not to add anything contrary to that which is plain. Notice also, he continued, the difference between the law and the gospel: 'The one axeth [asks] and requyreth, the wother perdoneth and forgeveth.'[12]

After briefly urging his readers to repent and believe the gospel, Tyndale turned his attention to 'them that are learned in Christianity'. If his language offends them he requests pardon, but reminds them that he had no one to copy and no one from the past to help him with his English. It was therefore open to future revision: 'Count it as a thynge not havynge his full shape.' Such a revision the translator promised to undertake as soon as possible. Over the next ten years, as an outlaw hunted at times by as many as five government agents, Tyndale slipped from city to city as he continued his work of translation and revision.

His style was rich, varied and earthy. Tyndale translated, as he had promised, for the ploughboy. His translation is accurate and his language is plain, which is why his work was so popular and enduring. He used 'formal equivalence' (varying the translation of the same word), for instance in Romans 13:7, 'Give to every man therefore his *due*; tribute to whom tribute *belongeth*, custom to whom custom is *due*, fear, to whom fear *belongeth*; honour to whom honour *pertaineth*.' One Greek word covers *belongeth*, *due*, *pertaineth*. Often he would paraphrase; 'God forbid' to translate a Greek phrase 'it cannot be' is Tyndale's invention and copied by the 1611 *King James Version* fifteen times. There was no formalised spelling until the eighteenth century and the word 'it' is spelled eight different ways in his 1526 edition! However, this was tidied up in subsequent revisions and Tyndale's spelling, through the Bible, significantly influenced standard English spelling. Tyndale provided the nation with an English New Testament, and later also

---

12 Above, p. 74.

with much of the Old Testament, that spoke to the heart of the ordinary man. Many of his phrases have remained part of our English heritage:

'Borne the burden and heat of the day' (Matthew 20:12).
'Take thine ease, eat, drink and be merry' (Luke 12:19).
'For in him we live, and move and have our being' (Acts 17:28).

So much of Tyndale is timeless in the way it speaks even to the twenty-first century. For example phrases such as, 'We have a way in through faith' (Romans 5:2) and, those who 'chop and change with the word of God' (2 Corinthians 2:17, NIV has 'peddle') resonate with any age. Tyndale was not aiming at literary style but readability; in the event, he achieved the second and moulded the first.

Here is a familiar passage from Tyndale's New Testament of 1526, and because it is one of his most beautiful translations, it is worth quoting in full. It is 1 Corinthians 13.

'Though I speake with the tonges of men and angels, and yet had no love, I were even as soundynge brasse: and as a tynklynge Cynball. And though I could prophesy, and vnderstode all secretes, and all knowledge: yee, if I had all fayth so that I coulde move mountayns oute of there places, and yet had no love, I were nothynge. And though I bestowed all my goddes to fede the poore, and though I gave my body even that I burned, and yet have no love, it profeteth me nothynge.

Love suffreth longe, and is corteous. Love envieth nott. Love doth nott frawardly, swelleth not, dealeth not dishonestly, seketh nott her awne, is not provoked to ange, thynketh not evyll reioyseth not in iniquitie: but reioyseth in the trueth, suffreth all thynge, beleveth all thynges hopeth all thynges, endureth in all thynges. Though that prophesyinge fayle, other tonges shall cease, or knowledge vanysshe awaye: yet love falleth never awaye.

For oure knowledge is vnparfet, and oure prophesyinge is vnperfet: but when thatt which is parfet is come: then that which is vnparfet shall be done awaye. When I was a chylde, I spake as a chylde, I vnderstode as a child, I ymmagened as a chylde: but as sone as I was a man I put awaye all childesshnes. Nowe we se in a glasse even in a darke speakynge: but then shall we se face to face. Nowe I knowe vnparfectly: but then shall I knowe even as I am knowen. Nowe abideth fayth, hope, and love, even these thre: but the chefe of these is love.'

One thing will be clear from reading this, and that is that the *King James Version* of 1611 was heavily dependent upon Tyndale. At least eighty per cent of its New Testament was copied almost straight from Tyndale's revision of 1534. The year following this revision, Tyndale was betrayed, taken to the Castle of Vilvorde, and in October 1536 he was strangled and burnt at the stake. History records that he died with the prayer: 'Lord, open the King of England's eyes.' Tyndale had not completed the Old Testament translation before his death.

In that same year two Bibles were circulating in England: one came from the pen of Miles Coverdale (who finished the Old Testament where Tyndale had left off), and the other, *Matthew's Bible*, from John Rogers. Rogers was later among the first to be burnt at Smithfield in 1555 by Queen Mary. He was an able translator and improved on Coverdale (who could not translate from the Hebrew or Greek), especially in the Old Testament. Both Bibles were dedicated to Henry VIII and awaited his royal assent. Both contained Tyndale's New Testament virtually unaltered and were heavily dependent upon his translation of the Pentateuch and parts of the rest of the Old Testament. The king ran his eyes over Coverdale's Bible. Tyndale's name did not appear, and the bishops assured him they could find no errors: 'Then if there be no heresies,' roared Henry, 'in God's name, let it go abroad among the people.'

On 5 September 1538 Henry ordered every church in England to display 'one book of the whole Bible of the largest volume in English', the cost to be borne equally by the parson and the parishioners. A small phrase of immense significance was added to the foot of the title page of *Matthew's Bible*: 'Set forth with the kinges most gracyous lycense.' The people were urged to learn the Lord's Prayer, the *Apostles' Creed* and the Ten

Commandments in English—for this, a woman and six labourers had been burnt at Coventry on 4 April 1519. Private copies of the New Testament were eagerly bought, and even by the year of Tyndale's martyrdom, one writer could conclude, perhaps with only marginal exaggeration, 'Every man hath a Testament in his hand.'

On 14 November 1539 Henry sent to all 'printers and sellers of books' a royal encouragement for the 'free and liberal use of the Bible in our own maternal English tongue'. As if to anticipate the king, Robert Redman was printing Tyndale's translation in 1538, and his print shop was next door to St Dunstan's in the City of London, where the great Reformer once preached.

The *Geneva Bible*—
the Bible of the Reformers and Puritans

The translations of Miles Coverdale (*Coverdale's Bible*) and John Rogers (*Matthew's Bible*) were circulating freely and with the king's permission by the start of the new decade in 1540.[13] Coverdale, on his own admission, had little knowledge of Hebrew or Greek and relied heavily upon Tyndale's work which, for obvious reasons, he did not dare admit; he translated much of the Old Testament from the German and Latin. It was, in fact, Coverdale's translation of the Psalms that entered the *Book of Common Prayer* in 1539 and stayed there even when the rest was updated. The version of John Rogers, which the king liked sufficiently to give it his royal licence, was a mixture of the work of Tyndale, Coverdale and Rogers. Rogers used the pen name of Thomas Matthew but at the end of Malachi the initials 'W.T.' appear, which may have been left in by oversight, or deliberately to indicate that the hand of the great Reformer and translator was behind the Old Testament.

With Bibles now circulating freely, Coverdale was given the task of revising *Matthew's Bible*, so that a single recognized edition could fulfil

---

13 Facsimiles are available today of the Wycliffe Bible (Lamp Post Inc. 2008); Tyndale 1526 (Hendrickson Publishers, 2008); Matthew's Bible 1537 (Hendrickson Publishers, 2009, and a modernised version from Baruch House Publishing, 2015), and the Geneva Bible 1560 (Hendrickson Publishers, 2007).

the royal command of 1538 that by a certain day a copy of the Bible should be placed in every parish church in the land under penalty of a fine of four times the cost of the Bible for every month of delay! This was the *Great Bible* of 1539, which, like its predecessors, was heavily dependent upon Tyndale.

Henry VIII died in 1547, and in the closing years of his life he turned against the movement for reform, ordering that the possession of translations by Tyndale or Coverdale should be punishable by death. But it was too late. The *Great Bible* containing the work of these two translators, remained in every parish church.

During the brief reign of Edward VI, several attempts were made to offer alternative translations, but they each came to nothing and the *Great Bible* held its ground. The reaction under Mary from 1553 to 1558, during which John Rogers along with almost three hundred men and women who remained faithful to the Reformation were burnt at the stake, had little or no impact upon the *Great Bible*, and by the accession of Elizabeth I in 1558 only the wear and tear of age had made inroads on the copies of the Bible in each parish church.

The killing times of 'Bloody Mary' had driven hundreds of good men abroad in a carefully organized 'evacuation'. Some of them met up in Geneva, the city of the Reformers which, in the view of John Knox of Scotland, was 'the most perfect school of Christ' since the days of the apostles. A few of the English exiles set to work on a new translation using the help given by the great scholar Theodore Beza. William Whittingham led the team and, a year before Mary died, they produced their New Testament. By 1560 the Old Testament was complete, and the *Geneva Bible* was born—named after the town in which it was conceived and printed.

The *Geneva Bible* used Tyndale as its basis and revised it with the aid of Beza's Latin version and the latest Greek text of Robert Estienne in 1550. Perhaps one of the most notable features of the *Geneva Bible*, which shouldered its way into first place over the next half-century, was the notes that accompanied it. These notes reflected the strongly Reformed theology of John Calvin's Geneva and played a large part in moulding the minds of its readers.

The introduction to this Bible translation, that for one hundred and forty years became the Bible of virtually all the Puritans, began:

'To the moste vertuous and noble Quene Elizabet, Quene of England, France, and Ireland, etc. Your humble subjects of the English Church at Geneva, with grace and peace from God the Father through Christ Jesus our Lord.'

The preface, dated 10 April 1560 includes the reminder:

'except God by his worde dyd reigne in the heartes and soules, all mans diligence and indeuors [endeavours] were of none effect: for without this worde we can not discern between iustice and injurie, protection and oppression, wisdome and foolishnes, knollage and ignorance, good and evil.'

The *Geneva Bible* became the Bible of the later Reformers, and the Puritans used nothing else. In Scotland Knox preached from it, and in 1579 a Scottish edition was the first Bible to be printed in Scotland. In England Milton and Bunyan read it avidly for their poems and books, and it was the only Bible Shakespeare knew. The Pilgrim Fathers took it with them to the New World in 1620, and the *Soldier's Pocket Bible*, that Oliver Cromwell issued to his army as late as 1643, contained extracts from the *Geneva Bible*. More than two hundred years later 50,000 copies were distributed to Federal soldiers in the American Civil War.

David Daniell notes that one hundred and forty new editions of the *Geneva Bible* were printed before 1644.[14] Its immense popularity is seen in the fact that it was still being printed over thirty years after the first edition of the *King James Version* in 1611. It was the *Geneva Bible*, more than any other, than provided the foundation for the Reformation in England and, by no means incidentally, moulded the English language. England may have been slow to enter the race for Bible translations, but by the end of the sixteenth century it had caught up with and overtaken Europe. In the last fifty years of the century one hundred and twenty new editions were

---

14 David Daniell, *The Bible in English* (Yale University Press, New Haven and London, 2003), p. 294.

published, and Daniell estimates that just under half a million copies of the Bible were printed in England—and that among a total population of around six million. To claim that the *Geneva Bible* moulded the course of English history and literature is not an exaggeration.

The *Geneva Bible* was the first English translation to use verse divisions, the first to use italics for words that have been added to the text to make clear the meaning, and the first to contain cross-references in the margins. Summaries were included at the beginning of each new chapter. Much of the Old Testament (from Job to Malachi)—which Tyndale did not reach before his death and which Coverdale translated from the Latin—was translated directly from the Hebrew for the first time.

The *Geneva Bible* included the *Apocrypha*, as in fact did most translations until the eighteenth century. However, the translators were careful to advise their readers that the *Apocrypha* is not received 'by common consent' to be read publicly in the churches, nor to prove any point of Christian religion unless it can be confirmed by the Scriptures; however, they are useful for furthering our knowledge of history and 'the instruction of godlie maners'.

There were four, what we would call 'appendices' at the close of the book: a table interpreting the proper names found in the Bible, a thematic index, a chronology from Adam to 1560 (almost exactly a century before Archbishop James Ussher worked at the same sum), and finally a chronology from Paul's conversion to his execution under the orders of Nero in 'AD 70'. Later editions added two 'right profitable and fruitful concordances'. Thirty-three illustrations, such as Noah's ark and Solomon's temple, including twenty-six woodcut engravings, embellished the *Geneva Bible*, and a few maps illustrated the Holy Land and even located the Garden of Eden.

Whittingham's (or more correctly Estienne's) New Testament verse division was retained and the Old Testament verses came from the Masoretes in the ninth century AD. Thus it was the first Bible to publish the verse divisions that we use today. The *Geneva Bible* was a study Bible: every book has a brief introduction, and every chapter a short statement of contents.

Marginal notes and cross-references, many of which are perceptive and all are helpful, fill (and often overflow) both outside and inside margins. For example, beside Genesis 1:3 the explanation for God creating light before the sun and the moon is given: 'the light was made before either sunne or moone was created: therefore we must not attribute that to the creatures that are God's instruments, which onely apperteneth to God.'

Some of the notes are clearly exposition. By Matthew 21:2 and the choice of a colt we read: 'By this entrie Christ wolde shewe the state and condition of his kingdome, which is farre contrarie to the pope and glorie of the worlde.'

Other notes are exegesis, a comment on Matthew 21:5 'daughter of Sion' informs us 'That is, the citie of Sion, or Jerusalem.' And the reader is offered a helpful lesson in grammar beside the same verse: we are informed that the phrase 'sitting upon an asse, and a colte, the fole of an asse', is 'a manner of speech called synechdoche, whereby two are taken for one.'

Still other notes are explanation. Verse 7 of the same chapter might confuse the reader since two animals are in view and yet the disciples 'put on them their clothes and set him thereon.' The problem is solved with the simple explanation 'he ridde on the fole and the dame went by.'

Many notes have a warm pastoral application. Beside Genesis 8:1 where we read that God remembered 'everie beast and all the cattel', the translators add: 'If God remember everie brute beast, what oght to be the assurance of his children?' And others reveal the strong Reformed theology of the translators working in Calvin's city. Beside Isaiah 53:1 and the phrase 'to whome is the arme of the Lord revealed?' they add the theologically loaded comment: 'Meaning that none can beleve, but whose hearts God toucheth with the virtue of his holie Spirit.'

Like so many translations both before and since, the translators struggled with Romans 3:25. Tyndale had consistently translated the Greek word *hilastèrion* by 'hath made a seat of mercy' (1526 and 1534); Geneva opted for the more straightforward, but hardly more accurate 'to be a reconciliation'. The *King James Version* got this one right half a century later: 'to be a propitiation'.

Learning from Tyndale, it was a Bible for the people. The Geneva translators strove for a version that read well publicly and was easy to understand. In the eighteenth century it was dismissively referred to as 'the breeches Bible' because in Genesis 3:7 'they sewed fig leaves together and made themselves breeches'—although they had simply taken this phrase from Wycliffe's translation.

If the *Geneva Bible* had not included the marginal notes, many of which were clearly 'Calvinistic' and some (though not as many as is sometimes suggested) were against the papacy, it might well have rendered the next two versions, the *Bishops' Bible* and the *King James Version*, unnecessary. But in so doing it would have lost both its value and appeal. Between 1560 and 1611 there were sixty-four editions of the 1560 *Geneva Bible* either as a whole or the New Testament. In 1576 Laurence Tomson, an Oxford graduate, revised the notes.

Meanwhile, from 1561, led by Archbishop Matthew Parker, the bishops had been busy with their own Bible which, unsurprisingly, was called the *Bishops' Bible* and, surprisingly, was ready by 1568. It suffered from being a hasty response to the *Geneva Bible* and one scholar has commented, 'For the most part the *Bishops' Bible* is either a lazy and ill-informed collection of what had gone before, or, in its original parts, the work of third-rate scholars and second-rate writers. In no way could it hold comparison with the *Geneva Bible*.'[15] In its short-lived day, it was never popular.

Although it was a fair revision of the *Great Bible*, it had already been outclassed by the greater ability of the translators of the *Geneva Bible* and could never catch up. The attempts to force it on the churches failed. Unfortunately, it was this *Bishops' Bible*, and not the *Geneva Bible*, that formed the basic text for the next revision to enter the stage.

The *King James Version*

A year after James I succeeded Elizabeth in 1603 he called a conference of leading churchmen and theologians at Hampton Court Palace to discuss

---

15 Quoted in *The Bible in English*. From Gerald Hammond, *The Making of the English Bible* (Manchester 1982), p. 143.

'things pretended to be amiss in the church'. The only result of this meeting worthy of note came right at the end, almost as a postscript. It was the resolution:

'That a translation be made of the whole Bible, as consonant as can be to the original Hebrew and Greek; and this to be set out and pointed [punctuated], without any marginal notes, and only to be used in all churches of England in time of divine service.'

This was the birth of the *Authorized Version*, or *King James Version*. In fact, it was no more King James' than Coverdale's Bible was King Henry's; it was never formally authorized by Parliament and the king had no hand in its work. But James was glad of any opportunity to get rid of the *Geneva Bible* with its notes which were, to his mind, far too Protestant and Reformed. After all, James was the son of Catholic Mary, Queen of Scots!

James arranged for six groups of translators to divide the work: three on the Old Testament, one on the *Apocrypha*, and two on the New Testament. Fifty-four scholars were chosen, although only forty-seven are known, and all were well qualified for their work. Unfortunately, it was to be a revision modelled on the *Bishops' Bible*; for this reason, it was in many respects a backward step from the *Geneva Bible* and those before it.

The *King James Version*, which was completed in 1611, reintroduced words that had a loaded ecclesiastical meaning in pre-Reformation days and had been abandoned by Tyndale and the *Geneva Bible*. For example, 'confess' was introduced in place of 'acknowledge' which appeared in both the *Geneva Bible* and in Tyndale's New Testament. 'Charity' was chosen in place of 'love', and 'church' in place of 'congregation'. At John 10:16 the translators chose, 'There shall be one *fold* and one shepherd'; years later the New Testament scholar Westcott referred to this as a 'disastrous' translation since it gave support to the Roman idea of one visible organized church on earth; although in this case even the *Geneva Bible* has 'sheepfold'. Tyndale (followed by all modern translations) had rightly translated it by the use of the word 'flock' referring to people. These may seem small issues today, but for many they were seen as a drift back to Rome. In fact, the translators were trying to steer a middle course, but whether they succeeded is a matter of opinion.

The *King James Version* was no stiff, word-by-word translation, although at times it was flat and unimaginative when, for example, it laboriously repeated a Hebrew phrase like 'And it came to pass' or discreetly used the phrase 'lay with' where Tyndale had more aptly translated 'slept with'. Occasionally, it could be accused of being too free: for instance, in Romans 5:2–3 the same Greek word appears as 'rejoice', 'glory' and 'joy' within the space of two verses; but Tyndale enjoyed that liberty. It is even open to the charge of paraphrasing: for example, in Matthew 27:44 the single Greek word 'revile' is rendered 'cast the same in his teeth', and Paul's expression, 'It cannot be' in Romans 6:15 is paraphrased as 'God forbid'—though we can blame Tyndale's 1526 New Testament for both these readings. In fact, the *King James Version*, like all its predecessors, was heavily dependent upon Tyndale and, as we have already noted, some eighty-three per cent of the New Testament matched Tyndale's 1534 revision and seventy-six percent of the Old Testament relied on Tyndale.[16]

Like every version before and after it, the *King James 'Authorized' Version* did not lack critics, particularly among those who were brought up on the *Geneva Bible*. The most vigorous of these was Dr Hugh Broughton, a recognized Hebrew and Greek scholar who was left out of the translation team possibly because of his abrasive character and because he was known to be working on his own revision of the *Geneva Bible*. Broughton hated the new translation and told the king so: 'The cockles of the sea shore, and the leaves of the forest, and the grains of the poppy, may as well be numbered as the gross errors of this Bible.' This charge is reminiscent of Bishop Tunstall who, within a few short months of Tyndale's New Testament arriving in this country, claimed to have found three thousand errors within its pages. It is hard to be an unprejudiced critic when we feel threatened!

Despite Hugh Broughton, and the strong supporters of the *Geneva Bible*, the *King James Version* slowly gained ascendancy over the *Geneva Bible* and remained at centre stage for the next three and a half centuries.

---

16 John Nielson & Royal Skousen, 'How much of the King James Bible is William Tyndale's? *Reformation*, 3 (1998), pp. 49–74. Ref. *The Bible in English*, p. 448.

However, the reason for this was not because of its merits. From the conference at Hampton Court Palace in 1603, by royal decree it was destined to be the Bible 'only to be used in all churches of England in time of divine service.' When successive publishers were given a monopoly for printing Bibles in England, it was the *King James Version* they were expected to promote. All others, the *Geneva Bible* especially, were thus squeezed out of a market that was rigged by the printers who had, with royal patronage (The King's Printers), invested heavily in this new Bible. Archbishop Laud prohibited any Bible with marginal notes; clearly the *Geneva Bible* was in his sights. Evidence of the *King James Version's* unpopularity is seen in the fact that the first printer, Robert Barker, who was granted a monopoly on its production, went bankrupt almost at once.

Eventually the printing of the *Geneva Bible* was forbidden and finally imports were banned. By 1644 the last *Geneva Bible* was printed in England, although some editions of the *King James Version* appeared with *Geneva Bible* notes. Controversially, but with good historical and linguistical reason, David Daniell insisted: 'The forcible replacement from 1611 of the remarkable, accurate, informative, forward-looking, very popular *Geneva Bibles* at the time of their greatest dissemination and power, with the backward-gazing, conservative KJV was one of the tragedies of western culture.'[17]

At first the *Apocrypha* was bound in with the *King James Version*, and in 1615 Archbishop Abbott forbade anyone to issue an edition without this inclusion. The Puritans objected, and the issue remained alive for many years; it is still possible to buy copies of the *King James Version* with the *Apocrypha*. The *King James Version* was the first complete Bible to be printed in North America in 1781.

Because the English language has changed considerably since 1611, the *King James Version* has been revised over the years. In 1769 it was updated by Dr Blayney, and the spelling of the 1611 edition would be oddly unreadable for a modern congregation. For comparison with Tyndale's

---

17 David Daniell, *The Bible in English*, p. 442.

1526 translation of 1 Corinthians 13 quoted earlier in this chapter here is the same passage in the exact words and spelling of the first edition of the *King James Authorized Version* in 1611:

1. Though I speake with the tongues of men & of Angels, and haue not charity, I am become as sounding brasse or a tinkling cymbal. 2. And though I haue the gift of prophesie, and vnderstand all mysteries and all knowledge: and though I haue all faith, so that I could remooue mountaines, and haue no charitie, I am nothing. 3. And though I bestowe all my goods to feede the poore,and though I giue my body to bee burned, and haue not charitie, it profiteth me nothing. 4. Charitie suffereth long, and is kinde: charitie enuieth not: charitie vaunteth not it selfe, is not puffed vp, 5. Doeth not behaue it selfe vnseemly, seeketh not her owne, is not easily prouoked, thinketh no euill, 6. Reioyceth not in iniquitie, but reioyceth in the trueth:7. Beareth all things, beleeueth all things, hopeth all things, endureth all things. 8. Charitie neuer faileth: but whether there be prophesies, they shall faile; whether there bee tongues, they shall cease; whether there bee knowledge, it shall vanish away. 9. For we know in part, and we prophesie in part.10. But when that which is perfect is come, then that which is in part shall be done away. 11. When I was a childe, I spake as a childe, I vnderstood as a childe, I thought as a childe; but when I became a man, I put away childish things. 12. For now we see through a glasse, darkely: but then face to face: now I know in part, but then shall I know euen as also I am knowen. 13. And now abideth faith, hope, charitie, these three, but the greatest of these is charitie.

The *Douai Bible*—a Bible for Roman Catholics

At first Rome was violently opposed to any suggestion that the people should have what John of Gaunt referred to as 'God's laws in their own language.' In the view of Rome, only the church could interpret the word of God. However, when that battle had been lost, it was considered wiser to approve a translation suitable for members of the Catholic community.

But Rome was slow to move. Because the New Testament was first published in 1582 while the college was still at Rheims, it is sometimes referred to as the *Rheims New Testament*. The full Bible was completed at Douai around 1610 by Gregory Martin, a Roman Catholic exile during the reign of Elizabeth and a member of the English College at Douai, Northern France.

The first principle was that the basic text for translating had to be the Latin *Vulgate* of Jerome. This was considered even better than the Greek 'in those places where they disagree'. This is still the first principle for any translation by Rome and therefore, strictly, Catholic versions of the Bible are revisions of a translation rather than new translations. The translators of the *Douai Bible* kept Latin words and even phrases and admitted to a word-for-word approach at times. This occasionally led to such unhelpful renderings as 'against the Spirituals of wickedness in the celestials' (Ephesians 6:12) and, complete nonsense to all who were without a Latin education: 'that you may be a new paste as you are Azymes' (1 Corinthians 5:7) and 'conquinations and spots, flowing in delicacies' (2 Peter 2:13) and much more of the same. Gregory Martin hoped that these Latin words would find their way into the English language; they did not. If a verb is not required in the Latin (or the Greek), it is not supplied in the English either, therefore Hebrews 13:4 became: 'Marriage honourable in all.' The Psalms contain some quite unintelligible phrases because here Jerome translated from the *Septuagint*; the *Douai* Psalms are therefore a revision of a translation from a translation of a translation! However, it must be admitted that in places even this Bible was significantly dependent upon Tyndale through Coverdale and the *Geneva Bible*—an irony indeed.

The marks of Roman theology are nevertheless evident. John and Jesus both call upon their hearers to 'do penance, for the Kingdom of heaven is at hand'. Our Lord prays that 'this chalice' might pass from him, and Paul and Barnabas ordain 'priests in every church'. The *Douai Bible* included the *Apocrypha*, except for the books of Esdras and the Prayer of Manasseh which were printed separately at the end. The commentary that ran alongside the text helped the faithful to interpret the Bible in a Roman way.

Bishop Richard Challoner revised the *Douai Bible* in the eighteenth century (1750) and this, with its considerable *King James Version* influence, lasted until the *Confraternity Version* in 1941. Even this was based upon the Latin *Vulgate*, although it was preceded by the commencement of the *Westminster Version of the Sacred Scriptures* in 1935 based upon the Hebrew and Greek texts.

By far the most popular English translation for Roman Catholics, partly because it is an official version, is that of Ronald A. Knox, called 'a translation from the Latin *Vulgate* in the light of Hebrew and Greek originals'. This was completed in 1949 but its great weakness was in being tied to a copy of the *Vulgate* authorized in 1592 and clearly not accurate in places.

It is not always appreciated that the *Jerusalem Bible* is a Roman Catholic translation. Published in 1966, the full version contains commentary notes to draw out Roman Catholic theology. For example, the note on Exodus 12 claims, 'The Jewish Passover becomes a rehearsal for the Christian passover, the Lamb of God, Christ, is sacrificed (the cross) and eaten (the Last Supper) ... The mystical re-enactment of this redemptive act becomes the central feature of the Christian liturgy, organized around the Mass which is at once a sacrifice and a sacrificial meal.' The notes are also clearly liberal: a note on Jonah dismisses Jonah as the author and claims the book was written at a late date, concluding, 'The late date is warning enough against any interpretation of the book as history.'

The *Jerusalem Bible* is of little value as a translation, though it is still widely used for reading in Roman Catholic churches. However, Roman Catholics are now permitted to use some modern translations.

Beyond the *King James Version*

From the seventeenth century, the Bible shaped not only the religious life of the nation but every aspect of life, from science to literature, the arts and politics. More than half the founders of the Royal Society (1660) were Puritans wedded to the Bible and the Christian faith; even Isaac Newton wrote a commentary on the book of Daniel. The novels and poetry of John Bunyan (*Pilgrim's Progress*), Daniel Defoe (*Robinson Crusoe*),

John Donne (his poetry, prose and essays), John Dryden (*Absalom and Ahithophel*) and John Milton (*Paradise Lost and Regained*), to name but a few, and the songs, ballads and madrigals of the seventeenth century were all hugely influenced by the Bible. Both sides in the English Civil War (1642–1645) took comfort and vindication from the Bible. The metrical psalms of Nahum Tate and Nicholas Brady in 1696 were based on the *King James Version* and were an instant success.

For half a century from the Restoration of the Monarchy in 1660 the *King James Authorized Version* nudged its way forward with many imprints but with barely any revision. That revision was needed, to correct its errors and deficiencies in translation, was recognised by many, but nothing was effectively accomplished. Meanwhile, The *Geneva Bible*, having been forced out of the print shops by the Royal Patronage of the *King James Version*, slowly lost its hold. Even the Puritans had little choice but to change their allegiance. When, until his death in 1653, William Gouge spent thirty-three years and one thousand sermons preaching through the epistle to the Hebrews for his congregation at Blackfriars in London, it was the *King James Version* he used for his text. The London publisher, Thomas Guy, made a personal fortune from selling the KJV and from this he founded and endowed the hospital in Southwark, London, that bears his name today. However, from 1777 the newly independent America was printing its own Bibles and the bottom fell out of a lucrative British export.

Although no new translations or major revisions of the *King James Version* entered the popular market, many editions did appear with notes and commentaries. Some, as we have seen, using the *Geneva Bible* notes. Thomas Scott, a deist Anglican clergyman who was led to a living faith in Christ by John Newton, published a commentary alongside the Bible text and this was especially popular from 1792.

By the time of the Evangelical Awakening in the middle of the eighteenth century the *King James Version* was the only Bible known from the cradle to the grave. The preaching of George Whitefield, John Wesley, John Newton and hundreds of others, used no other text. The plethora of solid Christian hymns in this period all found their inspiration from the same book, as did the oratorio *Messiah* from Handel and so much more in music and literature. However, many objected to using the words of Scripture in the context of public entertainment; John Newton was included in this, although he 'improved' the situation by preaching a series of sermons on Handel's texts.

From the nineteenth century, serious attempts were made at revisions and translations, and in the twentieth century the floodgates opened. Today there is a bewildering assortment available to the modern reader with little sign of the flow coming to an end.

See chapter 5 'Which translation?', for the continuing story of our Bible in English.

2. How old is the Old Testament?

Since the fall of Constantinople to Islam in 1453, scholars have been eager to discover the earliest manuscripts that lie behind all translations of the Bible. But how close to the originals are those manuscripts?

The Old Testament was written in Hebrew, except for a few small portions in Aramaic. Hebrew was the language of the Jews and, until around six hundred years after the birth of Christ, it was written without vowels and with no spacing between words. Genesis 1:1–2 in English and without vowels, punctuation or spacing would look like this:

NTHBGNNNGGDCRTDTHHVNSNDTHRTHNWTHRTHWSFRMLSSNDM
PTDRKNSSWSVRTHSRFCFTHDPNDTHSPRTFGDWSHVRNGVRTHWTRS

Hebrew is read from right to left, and without vowels it is known as 'unpointed' Hebrew. Over the centuries, from the time Moses first wrote the Pentateuch (Genesis to Deuteronomy), the shape of the Hebrew letters has changed considerably. Those illustrated here are the letters that have been generally used since the first century AD.

Genesis 1:1–5 in unpointed Hebrew

Although Hebrew was not written with vowels, the Jews knew how to pronounce words by the way they learned them in the school or synagogue. However, from the sixth century AD, generations of Masoretes—scholarly Jews working at Tiberias on the western shore of Galilee—gradually introduced vowels into the text. They also fixed the shape of Hebrew letters, and divided the Hebrew Scriptures into words and paragraphs.

בְּרֵאשִׁית בָּרָא אֱלֹהִים אֵת הַשָּׁמַיִם וְאֵת הָאָרֶץ׃ וְהָאָרֶץ
הָיְתָה תֹהוּ וָבֹהוּ וְחֹשֶׁךְ עַל־פְּנֵי תְהוֹם וְרוּחַ אֱלֹהִים מְרַחֶפֶת
עַל־פְּנֵי הַמָּיִם׃ וַיֹּאמֶר אֱלֹהִים יְהִי אוֹר וַיְהִי־אוֹר׃ וַיַּרְא
אֱלֹהִים אֶת־הָאוֹר כִּי־טוֹב וַיַּבְדֵּל אֱלֹהִים בֵּין הָאוֹר וּבֵין
הַחֹשֶׁךְ׃ וַיִּקְרָא אֱלֹהִים ׀ לָאוֹר יוֹם וְלַחֹשֶׁךְ קָרָא לָיְלָה וַיְהִי־
עֶרֶב וַיְהִי־בֹקֶר יוֹם אֶחָד׃

Genesis 1:1–5 in pointed Hebrew

The work of the Masoretes was completed by the tenth century. The vowels and punctuation were indicated as tiny dots and dashes within, under and after the letters. These marks, known as 'points', are therefore a mixture of punctuation and vowel signs to aid pronunciation.

The New Testament was originally written in Greek which, during the first few centuries of the Christian church, was the most widely spoken language across the Roman world and could rightly be called the language of the ordinary people—the *lingua franca* of the day. Although there are vowels in Greek, similar to those in English, punctuation was little better than in Hebrew, and in the early Greek texts there is almost no punctuation at all. Greek is read from left to right.

Βίβλος γενέσεως Ἰησοῦ Χριστοῦ, υἱοῦ Δαβίδ, υἱοῦ Ἀβραάμ.
Ἀβραὰμ ἐγέννησε τὸν Ἰσαάκ· Ἰσαὰκ δὲ ἐγέννησε τὸν Ἰακώβ·
Ἰακὼβ δὲ ἐγέννησε τὸν Ἰούδαν καὶ τοὺς ἀδελφοὺς αὐτοῦ· Ἰούδας
δὲ ἐγέννησε τὸν Φαρὲς καὶ τὸν Ζαρὰ ἐκ τῆς Θάμαρ· Φαρὲς δὲ ἐγέν-
νησε τὸν Ἐσρώμ· Ἐσρὼμ δὲ ἐγέννησε τὸν Ἀράμ· Ἀρὰμ δὲ ἐγέν-
νησε τὸν Ἀμιναδάβ· Ἀμιναδὰβ δὲ ἐγέννησε τὸν Ναασσών· Ναασ-
σὼν δὲ ἐγέννησε τὸν Σαλμών· Σαλμὼν δὲ ἐγέννησε τὸν Βοὸζ ἐκ τῆς
Ῥαχάβ· Βοὸζ δὲ ἐγέννησε τὸν Ὠβὴδ ἐκ τῆς Ῥούθ· Ὠβὴδ δὲ ἐγέννησε τὸν Ἰεσσαί· Ἰεσσαὶ δὲ ἐγέννησε τὸν Δαβὶδ τὸν βασιλέα.

The Greek text of Matthew 1:1–6

Writing materials for the first manuscripts

Apart from the Egyptian hieroglyphic symbols, the earliest hard evidence
of writing comes from southern Iraq shortly before 3,000 BC in the form of
cuneiform script. At first, all state documents were chipped onto stone or
pressed into clay tablets which were then baked hard in the sun. This was
a slow process, and the documents were large and heavy to store.

Leather (referred to as 'parchment'), from the skins of sheep, goats or
cattle, was lighter, very strong and long-lasting; and it was pliable so that
it could be rolled into a scroll without cracking. Vellum was a high-quality
leather made from calf-skin, although the young of sheep, goats or deer
were also used to produce vellum. Almost certainly the scrolls referred to
in Psalm 40:7; Jeremiah 36:23 and Ezekiel 2:9 were made of animal skins.
It was a rule that all copies of the Jewish Law should be written on leather.
One scroll reached 40.5 m (133 ft) in length, but generally 10.7 m (35 ft)
was a maximum. As a guide, the book of Isaiah would require more that
10 m (35 ft) of scroll, the Gospel of Luke 9.7 m (32 ft) and the entire New
Testament would be some 61 m (200 ft) in length.[18]

A much cheaper form of writing material than leather, and therefore
more common, was papyrus. This was made from the inner pith of the
papyrus plant that grew plentifully along the banks of the Nile river.

---

18 Sir Frederick Kenyon, *Handbook to the Textual Criticism of the New Testament*, 2nd ed.
(Eerdmans, Grand Rapids 1953), p. 35.

Thin strips of papyrus would be laid vertically and then another layer placed horizontally across them; the whole was pressed hard, dried in the sun and rubbed smooth. Papyrus was in use at least 3,000 years before the Christian church was born. Papyrus was the nearest material to our paper; it was cheap but flimsy: bright sunshine, a damp cave or nesting mice would soon destroy it. Another name for papyrus was *biblos* and a *biblion* was a roll of *biblos*; hence our word 'Bible' which literally means 'books'. The 'paper and ink' of 2 John 12 would be parchment and the ink was usually soot mixed with gum.

Whilst scrolls were at first the common form for storing writing, most of our Greek manuscripts are in the form of books or *codices* (singular: *codex*)—a word which comes from the Latin word *caudex*, a tablet. A large sheet of parchment or papyrus was folded and (sometimes) stitched together. Folded four times it produced an eight-page (quarto) codex and folded again produced a sixteen-page (octavo) codex. Thus, a scroll of ten metres or more, which was both clumsy and time-consuming to roll and unroll, was replaced by a 'book'. The text was more accessible, both sides could be written on, the content was fixed, and many documents could be bound together.

The first step from a scroll to a codex was a notebook produced by thin slivers of wood or parchment with holes punched at the bottom and held together with rings. It was, in effect, a 'ring-binder'. The Greeks had no word for this new progress and they used the Latin word *membranae* to identify it. Significantly, when Paul asked Timothy to bring him his scrolls and ' especially the parchments' (2 Timothy 4:13) the word translated 'parchments' is *membranas*. Paul was using notebooks.[19]

During the first century, the Christians were quick to adopt codices for their Scriptures, and by the fourth century nothing else was used. Generally, Jewish literature was written on parchment scrolls, pagan literature on papyrus scrolls, whilst the Christians preferred papyrus codices. Of all the New Testament papyri so far discovered, less than a

---

19 For an example of an early 'notebook' see Anderson and Edwards, *Evidence for the Bible* (Day One Publications, Leominster, 2014), p. 145.

handful are from scrolls. Clearly the Christians preferred to use codices because it was cheaper (both sides of the paper were used), easier to store, and more simple to locate a particular section than having to unroll a scroll.

A scroll of the entire New Testament would be impossible, and up to AD 300 it would even be most unlikely for all twenty-seven books to be contained within one codex because of the expense and bulk. The books circulated in clusters, beginning with the Gospels and followed by the apostles (Paul especially), and then Acts and the other letters, and finally the Revelation of John.

Copying the original manuscripts

The original texts of the Bible, both Old and New Testaments, are known as the 'autographs'. These would be the original manuscripts that were written as the prophet preached it or the apostle dictated it; for example, Jeremiah's scribe Baruch, or Peter's scribe Silas (Jeremiah 36:4; 1 Peter 5:12). We would not expect any of these to be available today because they were written on papyrus or parchment, which eventually wore out and copies were made. Almost all that we have are copies of copies many times over. These handwritten copies are known as 'manuscripts' from the Latin *manu scriptum* meaning 'written by hand'; the word is often abbreviated to MS, with the plural MSS.

See Book 1 chapter 6 in this series under 'The accuracy of the scribes' for more on the care in the transmission of the text.

Printing was not available until the fifteenth century. The Hebrew Old Testament was first printed in 1488 and the New Testament in Greek not until 1516. Before this, every copy of the original text, and every translation into another language, had to be written out by hand. Some assume that this is exactly where all the mistakes came in; they suggest that even if it had been originally free from error, as the centuries went by and more and more copies were made, so more and more mistakes entered the text. It is assumed, therefore, that by now it is quite impossible to claim that we have the words of Jeremiah or Peter for example.

That may sound convincing, but there is no ancient literature so well attested as the Bible, and with copies that are closer to the original autographs. Here are some comparisons:

• The Jewish scholar Josephus was a near contemporary of the apostles. The earliest complete text of his *Jewish Antiquities* (History of the Jews) is dated 1,300 years after his death.

• The earliest manuscripts available for the works of the Greek philosopher Plato who died around 350 BC are 1,200 years after his death.

• Julius Caesar wrote his own account of his campaigns in Gaul (France) from 58 to 55 BC. The earliest existing record of his *Gallic Wars* is 900 years after his death.

• Tacitus was a Roman historian and contemporary with the apostles. The earliest copies of his *Annals*, which covered the history of Augustus to Nero, and his *Historiae* of the Roman Empire from AD 69 to 97 are 800 years after his death.

In each case, we have only a few texts available to compare, but scores of copies must have been made in those intervening years.

By contrast, as we will see later in this chapter, we have copies of a complete New Testament made only 300 years after the death of the apostles, and many parts are confirmed from texts dating only a few decades from the apostles. In addition, there are available between 5,000 and 6,000 texts available for comparison plus thousands of very early translations (versions).

Even some of the Old Testament available texts, Isaiah is one, are as close to the originals as the existing copies of Tacitus are to his originals.

There are good reasons why we may be sure that we have an accurate Bible.

CARE IN COPYING THE OLD TESTAMENT

We have already noted how the Jewish Masoretes added the vowel 'points' to the Hebrew consonants so that future generations would be in no doubt as to exactly what the words meant and how they were to be pronounced. They continued their work into the tenth century AD. The word 'Masorete' comes from a word meaning 'to hand on' or 'transmit' and thus refers to 'tradition'. They were not authors, but were looking for what had always been accepted and they were careful not to alter the text of Scripture. The Masoretes built upon work already completed between AD 90 and 100 at a Jewish council at Jamnia, near the modern Tel-Aviv. This council confirmed both the books and the actual text of the Old Testament. The text with the vowel 'points' is known as the *Masoretic Text*. See in this series Book 3 chapter 2 under 'What happened at Jamnia?'

After the Masoretes had invented the dots and dashes of the Hebrew vowels, and divided the text into separate words, they had not finished. Their next task was to set down detailed rules to govern the transmission of the Scriptures. Some uninformed critics suggest that the scribes who copied out the Hebrew Scriptures carried on their work at odd moments, with only half a mind on their task, and with as little care as a child copying out a shopping list. We should remember that the scribes were not spare-time hobbyists; they were professionals who devoted their whole lives to the copying of the sacred texts, working together in a 'scriptorium'. Professor F F Bruce has described their care like this:

'They treated [the text] with the greatest imaginable reverence, and devised a complicated system of safeguards against scribal slips. They counted, for example, the number of times each letter of the alphabet occurs in each book; they pointed out the middle letter of the Pentateuch and the middle letter of the whole Hebrew Bible, and made even more detailed calculations than these ... and they made up mnemonics by which the various totals might be easily remembered.'[20]

Another scholar summarised the work of the scribes: 'Everything countable seems to be counted.'[21] The size of the scrolls to be used was carefully recorded; the width of columns, spaces between words and letters, even the colour of the ink and the clothing to be worn by the scribe were all given in detail. The scribe would have to submit his manuscript

---

20 F F Bruce, *The Books and the Parchments* (Pickering & Inglis Ltd, London 1950), p. 115.
21 Wheeler Robinson, *The Bible in its ancient and English versions* (1940), p. 29.

for checking and if it was in error at any point then it was ordered to be destroyed; he must start again.

Occasionally a scribe might think that he had found an error in the copy before him, but even then he was not allowed to make any alteration. Instead he would write the Hebrew word *kethib* ('it is written') above the suspect word and add his suggested correction in the margin under the word *kere* ('it should be read'). Sometimes these two words would distinguish between what was written and what should be read aloud in the synagogue. For example, the letters YHWH spell the word for the divine name revealed to Moses in Exodus 6:2–3, it appears as LORD in our modern English translations. It was a holy name for Israel and they were reluctant to pronounce it, partly to avoid pagan nations applying it to their gods. Therefore, they substituted the common word *adonay* (lord or master) and placed the vowels of this word to the consonants of YHWH. The words *kethib* and *kere* would tell the reader that YHWH was written, but *adonay* should be read. When William Tyndale came across this hybrid word for his Old Testament translation he invented the word 'Jehovah', which has stayed with us.[22] Today, it is generally considered that the original vowels to YHWH were *a* and *e*—hence the often-used pronunciation *Yahweh*.

The Masoretes collected the variant readings they discovered in the Old Testament, most of which were very minor and made little difference to the meaning, and they amounted to about 1,200—that is, one and a half words for each chapter of our Old Testament.

There is a good reason why few very old manuscripts are in existence today. When one copy had been carefully checked, and found to be accurate in every detail, the older and fragile copy from which it was taken would be set aside in a room (known as a *genizah*) for old manuscripts and later buried in sacred ground. This was done to avoid a poor-quality copy from being used again. In a copy torn with age, a reader might be tempted to add his own words to the parts that were missing or were too faded to be read.

---

22 Wycliffe used the word *adonay*.

This detailed care by the Jewish scribes should give every impartial reader of the Bible confidence that what he has before him is overwhelmingly as God first gave it. There are a few small mistakes that, despite such care, did find their way into the text. See Book 5 chapters 4 and 5 in this series for more on these supposed 'errors'. Importantly, the oldest Hebrew texts available today from around AD 200 to 500 (that is, before the Masoretes started their work) show little variation (apart from spelling and grammar) from the Masoretic texts. See below for the *Dead Sea Scrolls*.

It may be relevant to comment here how the Israelites guarded their ancient Hebrew language throughout their varied history. After four hundred years in Egypt, they came out speaking and writing—not Egyptian—but Hebrew. Later, whether in exile in Assyria (eighth century BC), Babylonia (sixth century BC) or Persia (sixth century BC on) they held fast to their traditional language. And when their homeland was occupied by the Greeks and their Scriptures were translated into the common language of Greek (the *Septuagint* in the third century) or the Romans imposed Latin as the official language (first century on), the Jews never wavered in maintaining Hebrew as their spoken language and the language of their Scriptures—right up to the present day.[23] Their language was not a language to be lost, any more than their Scriptures were to be tampered with.

Texts for the Old Testament

HEBREW MANUSCRIPTS—THE *MASORETIC TEXT*

The Hebrew text of our Old Testament achieved its final form around AD 100 at the Council of Jamnia; the Masoretes from the seventh century added the vowel points. Since the Masoretes possessed much older copies of the Old Testament, they destroyed them when the new and highly accurate copies were made, to avoid old and damaged copies influencing future scribes.

---

23 See for example the article by Jan Joosten, 'How Hebrew became a Holy Language', *The Biblical Archaeological Review*, Jan/Feb 2017, Vol. 43, no. 1, pp. 44–49,62.

Until 1947—and the importance of this year will be seen later in this chapter—the oldest Hebrew manuscripts known to exist came from the ninth century AD. The oldest copy of a complete Hebrew Old Testament is the Leningrad Bible dated AD 1008. This forms the basis for the standard text used today in Kittel's *Biblia Hebraica*. It is generally agreed that even by the second century AD the Hebrew text 'had reached a high level of standardization'.[24] In fact, the Masoretes were only establishing the form of the Old Testament text in the same way that Muslim scholars were working on the text and pronunciation of the Qur'an. They would never think of adding to the ancient texts.[25]

The accuracy of the work of the Masoretes is illustrated by the agreed fact that their text was clearly the same as that used by Jewish writings and the early church leaders (Origen's *Hexapla* for example) centuries before the Masoretes began their work. The close agreement of the *Masoretic Text*, the Greek *Septuagint* and the text of the Hebrew *Dead Sea Scrolls* is also a part witness to the accuracy of the Hebrew Old Testament. As was noted above, with all the Hebrew texts available to them the Masoretes collected the variations, which amounted to around 1,200 mostly in single words. This was a little over one for every chapter in our Old Testament.

In 1939 Sir Frederick Kenyon, at one time Director of the British Museum, commented rather hopelessly: 'There is, indeed, no probability that we shall ever find manuscripts of the Hebrew text going back to a period before the formation of the text which we know as Masoretic.' How wrong a scholar can be we shall see later.

THE *SAMARITAN PENTATEUCH*

There is one Hebrew text that does not come from the 'family' of texts used by either the Masoretes or the Council of Jamnia. It is known as the *Samaritan Pentateuch*, and was discovered in 1616; the oldest copy is dated to the tenth century AD. For historical reasons that we need

---

24 Karen Jobes and Moisés Silva, *Invitation to the Septuagint* (Baker Academic, Ada, MI 2000), p. 147. They acknowledge that the slight variations in texts 'have no effect on the meaning of the text'.
25 Bruce, *The Books and the Parchments*, p. 116.

not trouble with here, the Jews and Samaritans lived as bitterly opposed neighbours from at least the division of the kingdom under Rehoboam in the tenth century BC. The Samaritans worshipped separately and made their own copies of the first five books of the Bible (the Pentateuch); they were not interested in the rest, since it was largely concerned with the history of Judah.

The *Samaritan Pentateuch*, which was written in Hebrew, had been deliberately altered in many places to suit Samaritan ways of worship and customs. However, although the changes amount to about 6,000 differences from the *Masoretic Text*, most of these are 'small and unimportant' matters of grammar or spelling.[26] The value of this text is that it is quite independent of the *Masoretic Text* and obviously came from a different 'family' of manuscripts. It agrees exactly with the *Masoretic Text* in the overwhelming proportion of the work; many critical scholars allow only around thirty-five occasions where the Samaritan text is equal to, or to be preferred to, the Masoretic.

VERSIONS (TRANSLATIONS) OF THE OLD TESTAMENT—THE *SEPTUAGINT*
Although translators may make a mistake, the value of the versions is that it can often be discovered what text they were using as a basis for their translation. The most important version of the Old Testament is the *Septuagint*. This is a Greek translation of the Hebrew Old Testament produced in Egypt. With the conquests of Alexander the Great after 323 BC taking in over two million square miles on three continents,[27] the Greek language became the common tongue. Jews were scattered all over the Greek-speaking world—the 'diaspora' as it is known— and many clung tenaciously to their Hebrew language. However, the Egyptian Pharaoh Ptolemy Philadelphus (285–246 BC) asked for copies of the Jewish Scriptures to be sent to Alexandria, accompanied by scholars who could translate them so that he could add these writings to his magnificent library. The Jewish leaders in Jerusalem obliged,

---

26 Bruce, *The Books and the Parchments*, p. 125.
27 The Roman Empire was more than twice this and the British Empire eventually covered 13 million square miles.

and despatched a copy of the Scriptures, written in letters of gold it is claimed, together with seventy-two learned men to undertake the work of translation. The result was known as the *Septuagint* from the Latin word for seventy. It is frequently identified simply by the Roman numeral LXX.[28]

The original translators probably limited themselves to the Pentateuch, but it is fairly certain that the whole Old Testament was complete by the middle of the second century BC. The *Septuagint* at once became the Bible of the Greek-speaking synagogues and, what is even more important for us, it was the version frequently used by the early Christians. The Old Testament was now easily accessible to the Gentile world. Many of the New Testament quotations taken from the Old Testament are based upon the *Septuagint* (see Book 2 chapter 4 in this series for the way the apostles used the *Septuagint*).

Of interest to us is the fact that the *Septuagint* is based upon Hebrew texts in existence at least eight hundred years before the *Masoretic Text* was established. However, as with any translation, it is not always possible to be sure of the Hebrew word being translated. Also, among the many copied manuscripts of the *Septuagint* available today, it is evident from their differences that a variety of texts were used at different times, and sometimes translation was done carelessly. Almost all the available copies, often little more than fragments, were copied by early Christians, and very occasionally they were guilty of adding a Christian theme to the text. Apparently, a text of the *Septuagint* used by Justin around AD 135, but which has not come down to us, added the words *'from the tree'* to Psalm 96:10 to make it a Messianic promise: 'Say among the nations, "The LORD reigns *from the tree*."'[29]

The *Septuagint* was valuable in providing the writers of the New Testament with 'ready-made' and understood words to explain the gospel in an Old Testament context. For example, 'propitiation' (*hilastèrion* in Romans 3:25), is presented in its Old Testament rather than pagan

---

28 For a full introduction, see above, *Invitation to the Septuagint* by Karen Jobes and Moisés Silva.
29 Justin, *First Apology*, Ch. 41.

context. For this reason, the apostles occasionally chose to follow the Greek translation because it clarified an otherwise obscure expression for the readers unfamiliar with the old covenant. In Hebrews 10:5, 'A body you prepared for me', is taken from the Greek of Psalm 40:6. The Hebrew reads: 'My ears you have pierced.' This is a reference to the bond-slave of Exodus 21:6 and was a familiar Jewish custom that had no meaning to a Gentile reader. The *Septuagint* paraphrased by using the whole (a body) in place of the part (an ear). The two expressions are complementary, not contradictory. This is an issue familiar to anyone translating the Bible or preaching from it; Paul adopted the paraphrase.

The *Masoretic Text* is to be preferred, partly because of the known care among the Jewish scribes in copying their Hebrew texts and the evident carelessness of some *Septuagint* scribes,.

OTHER VERSIONS

The *Septuagint* was not the only Greek version of the Old Testament. One produced by Aquila, a Jewish proselyte in first half of the second century, followed the Hebrew text literally, but did not gain widespread acceptance. Another by Theodotion, also a proselyte to Judaism, was based on an old Greek translation. Its only significance for us is that the early churches mainly used his version of Daniel for their Greek Old Testament. Lucian of Antioch produced a Greek text of the Old Testament that was used by Erasmus in the sixteenth century. There were others Greek versions, but it was the *Septuagint* that formed the main text of the Old Testament for the early Christians.

A Syriac version known as the *Peshitta*, or 'simple' version, also includes the New Testament. It was completed at the very latest by the end of the third century AD and one copy available bears the date AD 464. This is the oldest copy of the whole Bible, in any language, for which the date is certainly known. Unfortunately, the *Peshitta* is often more of a paraphrase than a translation and therefore it does not help the search for an accurate text.

Several Coptic versions were produced around the second and third centuries AD. Coptic was the language spoken in Egypt by the end of the first century AD. Once again, both Old and New Testaments are translated, but since the Old Testament was evidently based upon the *Septuagint*, the Coptic versions are of no help in discovering the Hebrew text. There are also versions from Ethiopia, Armenia, Georgia (in the Caucasus), Slavonia and others, but they are all based upon the *Septuagint*.

With the annexation of Greece as part of the Roman Empire in the middle of the second century BC, Greek became virtually the second language of the Empire. Although the civil service operated through Latin, virtually the whole of cultural and social life was in Greek. For this reason, all the earliest texts, whether the writings of the church leaders or the fragments of Scripture, are in Greek. From AD 180, Irenaeus wrote his monumental treatise against the heretics in Greek, and yet he was bishop of Lyons in Gaul (France). For more on Irenaeus see in this series Book 3 chapters 5 and 7. Across Western Europe, therefore, there was little need for the Gospels and letters of the apostles to be translated into Latin. As late as AD 200 Hippolytus of Rome was still using Greek for his valuable Christian writing.

One of the greatest theologians of the early Christian communities was Origen of Alexandria and later Caesarea. Before the year AD 250 he had produced a mammoth study of many Old Testament biblical texts available in his day. It is known as the *Hexapla*, meaning 'sixfold' because in six columns he placed side by side the Hebrew text, the same transliterated into Greek letters, then two versions of the Greek translation (Aquila and Symmachus), his own Greek translation, and finally Theodotion's Greek translation. In places, more columns were added. Unfortunately, most of the *Hexapla* did not survive the ravages of the Islamic invasion of Palestine in the seventh century.

The situation was different in North Africa where Latin was the common language. Souter is confident that 'In Tertullian's time a Latin New Testament already existed in Africa.'[30] That is early in the third

---

30 Alexander Souter, *The Text and Canon of the New Testament* (Duckworth & Co., London 1913), p. 36.

century. However, the reference to a 'New Testament' does not mean that we have a neat twenty-seven books edition. All that remains are parts of most of the books from the New Testament from a variety of texts. But it is sufficient to suggest that most of the canon, if not all, was circulating in Latin across North Africa at this time.

The only other versions to note are those of the Latin translations and particularly the work of Eusebius Hieronymus (Jerome) between AD 390 and 404. Jerome had no doubt in his mind that the Hebrew text was more reliable than the *Septuagint*, and his Old Testament in Latin clearly shows that he had access to the Hebrew texts which would be used by the Masoretes two centuries later. His translation is known as the *Vulgate* because it was written in the common (vulgar) tongue which was Latin. This became the standard text for many centuries, and our earliest English versions, including John Wycliffe's translation in the fourteenth century, were translated from the *Vulgate*.

There can be little doubt that the *Masoretic Text* reflects the oldest and most accurate text that formed the Jewish Old Testament. Both Origen early in the third century and Jerome late in the fourth century, rejected the *Septuagint* in preference for the Hebrew text that clearly formed the basis for the Masoretes' work. All our Bible translators from the *King James Version* up to the present time have followed Origen and Jerome in this judgement. There are a few places where the *Masoretic Text* is not easily understood and where the *Septuagint* may help. The areas of conflict between the versions and the *Masoretic Text* form only a tiny fraction of the whole of the Old Testament. See chapter 4 for a few examples of this.

However, for years a problem lay in the fact that our oldest existing Hebrew manuscript of the Old Testament was dated somewhere around the ninth century AD and that left a long time for possible errors to have crept in after the original manuscripts were written. Kenyon's hopeless conclusion that 'there is no probability' that we would ever find Hebrew manuscripts older than the *Masoretic Text* appeared to be a statement of fact. Then, as the dust of the Second World War began to settle, an incredible discovery was made.

The *Dead Sea Scrolls*

The story goes that during the summer of 1947 a Bedouin shepherd boy was searching for a lost goat between Bethlehem and the Dead Sea. Slipping into the shade of a large rock, he rested himself and idly tossed a stone into the narrow opening of one of many caves scattered about the barren wilderness of the Dead Sea. Suddenly, the boy sat upright and began to throw more stones into the cave; what he heard was not the thud he had expected, but a hollow ring of pottery. That discovery laid bare some of the most amazing finds ever made by archaeologists. Over the next few years thousands of scrolls, in various stages of decay and preservation, were discovered, all carefully wrapped and stored in pottery jars.

The owners of the scrolls are generally thought to have been the Essenes, a religious community of devout Jews who, between 130 BC and AD 68, lived in a large settlement, the remains of which have been discovered at Qumran. It is thought they hid their library of valuable documents in caves by the Dead Sea to protect them from the Romans after the destruction of Jerusalem in AD 70. Some recent research questions this identification of the community and suggests that the site at Qumran was a wealthy fortified manor house on a large agricultural estate and had little or nothing to do with the scrolls found in caves by the Dead Sea—and that the scrolls belonged to Sadducees and not Essenes.[31]

Whatever the outcome of this debate, the area in which they were found is known as Wadi Qumran so, whoever they belonged to, we can refer to them as the Qumran scrolls. Between them, eleven caves produced 40,000 manuscript fragments. These represented five hundred separate scrolls, a few of which were almost perfect and undamaged. One hundred of these scrolls were parts of the Bible, and altogether every Old Testament book except Esther is represented among the *Dead Sea Scrolls*.

At another site, a few miles distant, at Wadi Murrabba't, a garrison of Jewish rebels had been stationed before they were finally crushed by the Roman legionaries in AD 135. There were military despatches, personal letters and parts of the Old Testament. Some of these manuscripts had

---

31 *Biblical Archaeological Review*, 'Qumran in light of Ramat Hanadiv', March/April 2005.

been deliberately torn up, either by the escaping rebels or by the victorious Romans, and others had been used by rats, mice and birds for nesting materials. But here were Hebrew texts of the Old Testament, from the same family as the *Masoretic Text*, but going back to the second century AD.

In the Dead Sea caves a complete scroll of Isaiah was found. This scroll was written between 175 and 150 BC. The prophet Isaiah was preaching just over seven hundred years before Christ, so the gap between the original manuscript (734 BC) and our now earliest existing copy of it (about 150 BC) has narrowed to six hundred years. That may still seem a long time but previously our earliest existing copy was a *Masoretic Text* of AD 900. We now have Hebrew manuscripts almost one thousand years older than the existing copies of the *Masoretic Texts*!

In the chapter 4 we will compare the Qumran and Masoretic texts, but sufficient here to note that—spelling, grammar and punctuation aside— there is overwhelming agreement between them, even though separated by almost a thousand years.

With the Dead Sea texts, we have gone back almost one thousand years before the earliest existing copy of the Masoretic text. It is fair to claim that if that one thousand years showed such detailed accuracy and care in copying the manuscripts, then the same accuracy would be expected for the previous six hundred years from Isaiah's 'autograph' to the Dead Sea copy. Professor F F Bruce concluded: 'The new evidence [from the *Dead Sea Scrolls*] confirms what we had already good reason to believe—that the Jewish scribes of the early Christian centuries copied and recopied the text of the Hebrew Bible with the utmost fidelity.'[32]

---

32 F F Bruce, *Second Thoughts on the Dead Sea Scrolls* (Paternoster Press 1956), p. 62.

3. How old is the New Testament?

The situation with the New Testament is somewhat different from the Old Testament. Although many of the early Christians copied the New Testament books with great care, it is also true that some did not.

Often it was not their fault. There was a great demand for the Gospels and letters; copies were needed urgently to instruct young churches and every copy had to be produced by hand without the discipline of the Jewish scriptorium. Often Christians carried on this work with constant interruptions during the years of severe persecution. In AD 303 the Roman Emperor Diocletian ordered all the sacred books of the Christians to be burned; consequently, the New Testament must have become scarce and in great demand. However, we can have confidence in the accuracy of our New Testament text for several reasons.

The copies that we do possess are close in time to the original autographs; some small portions are separated by only a few decades from the originals. Also, we have literally thousands of portions of New Testament texts and so, by comparing them, it is much easier to discover the original text. If five children are asked to copy a sentence from the school wallboard, and only three produce identical copies, we might not be sure whether the three are right, or whether they made the same mistakes by coincidence. But if 500 copied the sentence and 300 were identical and the others disagreed among themselves, we could be certain of the original text. It is something like this with the large number of New Testament texts available to us.

Sometime after AD 325, the Emperor Constantine, having embraced the Christian faith, ordered copies of the New Testament to be produced, and we know that great care was taken in their production. The majority of differences between the available texts are due to unintentional errors. However, Bruce Metzger draws attention to the evidence of the 'careful and painstaking work on the part of many faithful copyists'.[33]

One thing we can be sure of is that not one part of Christian teaching is dependent upon a verse that has conflicting texts behind it. It is sometimes assumed that the New Testament is full of contradictory readings and that to talk of an errorless text is nonsense in the light of this. Some critics toss about frightening figures of up to a quarter of a million 'textual variants' in the New Testament. This is wholly misleading, even to the point of dishonesty. The fact is that ten small differences in the spelling of words may be copied into fifty other texts; this is counted as five hundred 'textual variants', whereas it is only ten variations copied faithfully fifty times. Most of the variants are at the level of spelling differences, and it is hardly surprising that two thousand years ago copyists had problems with spelling. As we saw in chapter 1, in his English translation of the New Testament in 1526, William Tyndale managed to spell the word 'it' eight different ways throughout the New Testament—three in Matthew 5:34–35 alone—and it would be dishonest to accuse Tyndale of seven 'errors' over that variation.

Dr Brooke Westcott was bishop of Durham during the nineteenth century and, though not committed to an inerrant Bible, is still recognised as an excellent scholar of the New Testament Greek text. Together with his colleague, Dr Fenton Hort, they compiled what they believed to be the correct text of the New Testament. In doing so they researched every known text available at the time and concluded that the amount of the New Testament where there is any significant variation in the various sources 'can hardly form more than a thousandth part of the entire text'.[34] That 'thousandth part of the entire text' is not unimportant, but this figure is reassuring. However, our belief in an errorless Bible demands that we treat every possible discrepancy with seriousness.

---

33 For a few examples of both unintentional and intentional errors see Metzger, *The Text of the New Testament*, pp. 186–206.
34 B F Westcott, *The New Testament in the Original Greek*, p. 2.

Where did the chapters and verses come from?

The chapter and verse divisions of both the Old and New Testaments are not part of the original Scripture. Isaiah and Paul were no more concerned to divide their material into chapters and verses than we are when we write a letter, text or email. Some of these divisions in our Bibles can be misleading when they break into the writer's flow unnaturally.

The earliest existing copies of the Hebrew Old Testament that we possess are manuscripts of the prophet Isaiah and these copies are dated about 150 BC among the *Dead Sea Scrolls*. They contain an old system of indicating paragraph divisions using Hebrew letters; however, these divisions are not the same as we find in our Bible today. The verse divisions of the Old Testament appear to be older than the chapter divisions. The present verse division of the Old Testament was established by the Masoretes by AD 900. It is generally concluded that chapter divisions of the Old Testament were introduced by Cardinal Hugo de Sancto Caro in 1244,[35] although it would appear they were in the Latin Old Testament of Stephen Langton who was appointed Archbishop of Canterbury in 1207. Some authorities suggest they were incorporated into the Hebrew Bible by Rabbi Salomon Ben Ishmael about 1330.

Some of the early Greek manuscripts of the New Testament contained a form of chapter divisions. *Codex Vaticanus*, for example, was copied sometime in the fourth century and there are one hundred and seventy divisions in Matthew alone; *Codex Alexandrinus* had a completely different system of dividing the text (see below for these). However, neither of these form our present chapters.

The chapter divisions of the New Testament were added by Cardinal Hugo de Sancto Caro in 1244 and the verse divisions were introduced by Robert Estienne into his 1551 edition of the Greek New Testament. William Tyndale's New Testament of 1526 (revised in 1534) contained our chapters but not verse divisions, and the same was true of the New Testament of the *Geneva Bible* which was printed in Geneva in 1557. Verses were first introduced into an English translation of the New Testament

---

35 F F Bruce, *The Books and the Parchments* (Pickering & Inglis, London 1950), p. 118.

by Whittingham in that same year, and all English translations since then have followed our familiar pattern of chapter and verse divisions. The first complete Bible to contain our present chapter and verse divisions for both the Old and New Testaments was the *Geneva Bible* published in 1560.

The New Testament manuscripts

The amount of material available for discovering our New Testament Greek text is enormous. It needs to be, because many of the manuscripts of the New Testament were copied in a hurry and mistakes crept in easily. But before we find out how much is available and how reliable it all is, we must discover the type of material that exists today.

Just as the *Masoretic Text*, compiled from the seventh century, formed the basic text for our Hebrew Old Testament, so the *Textus Receptus* (coded as ω) or *Received Text*, compiled in the sixteenth century, for many years formed the basic text for our Greek New Testament. There was little biblical Greek scholarship in Western Europe before AD 1453; in that year Constantinople fell to the armies of Islam, and Christian scholars fled to the west with priceless Greek manuscripts. During the next century, many editions of the Greek New Testament were produced. Before this time the only Bible allowed was the Latin translation of Jerome (the *Vulgate*), but even Jerome used mainly Latin texts for his work and only a few Greek manuscripts.

In March 1516 Desiderius Erasmus, a Dutchman and one of the greatest Greek scholars of the sixteenth century, published a Greek New Testament based on a variety of manuscripts dating from the eleventh to the fourteenth centuries. At places, Erasmus lacked any Greek text and simply retranslated from the Latin *Vulgate*; in other places his texts were clearly in error, but overall it was a sound piece of editing with the material available. 1 John 5:7–8 was originally left out since no Greek manuscript contained it, but it was later inserted on the single authority of a supposed fifteenth century text (possibly written to order).

This first edition was followed by many other editions, all using Erasmus as a basis, but with access to other Greek manuscripts as they became available. Erasmus himself issued his fourth and final edition in 1527. This formed the basis for William Tyndale's revised English New Testament in 1534. It was an edition printed by Robert Estienne (often referred to as Stephanus or Stephens) of Paris in 1550, that became known as the *Received Text*. Estienne printed some of the variant readings from Greek texts in the margin. Estienne used Erasmus' work, that of Cardinal Ximenes, and about sixteen Greek manuscripts. The Greek text of Estienne was the basis for the *King James Authorized Version* in 1611. (See also the next chapter under The *Received Text*.)

GREEK TEXTS

Since the time of Erasmus and Estienne, literally thousands of Greek manuscripts, some of them only fragments, have been discovered and these have all added to our production of an accurate New Testament text. Currently there are over 5,800 Greek texts that have been catalogued and available to scholars, from fragments to complete New Testaments. Only fifty complete copies of the Greek New Testament have survived, and of individual books, Revelation is the least well represented, being found in around three hundred manuscripts. Rarely was the entire New Testament contained in one book because it would be far too bulky and expensive, and for this reason we hardly expect to find more than portions of it in one volume.

UNCIALS* AND *CODICES

Just under three hundred of the available Greek texts are in the 'uncial' form, a word meaning that they were written with letters similar to our capitals; sometimes referred to as 'majuscules'. Each letter was separated from its neighbour, and the text had all the appearance of clean and careful scribal copying. All works of literature were written in uncial because it was the style of the scholar. Generally, our oldest texts are the uncials, and therefore we do not have so many of them. Just under three hundred of the available texts are in the uncial form. Naturally these carefully scribed and separated letters took up a lot of space when both papyrus and parchment were scarce and expensive, they also took more time and care to copy.

Some of the best known uncials are these (in brackets is the code by which they are known):

Codex Sinaiticus (ℵ) was discovered in the mid-nineteenth century at a monastery on Mount Sinai by Constantin von Tischendorf from the University of Leipzig. It originally contained the whole Old Testament plus six books of the *Apocrypha*, though parts had been destroyed with age before the book was rescued. Apart from this, it is in excellent condition and contains the whole of the New Testament. The *Epistle of Barnabas* and the *Shepherd of Hermas* (three-quarters destroyed) are added at the end, separated from the canon. *Sinaiticus* was originally copied in Alexandria, found its way to the monastery on Sinai, was sold to Alexander II, the Tsar of Russia, and purchased in 1933 from the communist authorities in the Soviet Union jointly by the British Government and the British Museum for £100,000. It is now in the British Library. *Sinaiticus* is the only known complete copy of the New Testament in uncial script. It is dated around the middle of the fourth century AD.

According to Eusebius, the church historian and spiritual advisor to the emperor Constantine, around the year AD 331 the emperor ordered 'fifty copies of the sacred Scriptures' to be produced on fine parchment and with the utmost attention to accuracy. They were duly presented to him 'magnificently and elaborately bound'.[36] Some scholars have suggested that *Sinaiticus* may well have been one of those fifty Bibles. However, the addition of Hermas and Barnabas at the end questions this because Eusebius listed those two as rejected books.

Codex Vaticanus (B) has been in the Vatican since late in the fifteenth century, but even Erasmus was not allowed to use it. It also comes from Alexandria and contains both the Old Testament and the New Testament (together with most of the *Apocrypha*) although the beginning and the end are missing; it ends at Hebrews 9:14. *Vaticanus* may be even older than *Sinaiticus*, and some prefer this as one of those

---

36 Eusebius, *The Life of Constantine*, IV. 36.

fifty copies referred to above. It is considered by some scholars to be the best Greek text we have of the New Testament.

Codex Alexandrinus (A) was presented to King Charles I of England by the Patriarch of Alexandria in 1627. Written somewhere between AD 350 and 450, it originally contained the whole Old and New Testaments (including the *Apocrypha*), though much for the New has been destroyed through age. Copied in the fourth or fifth centuries, like *Sinaiticus*, it is in the British Library. The only 'rogue' books present are 1 and 2 Clement, which is odd since they were not in general use by the fourth century.

These three represent what is known as the Alexandrian school (or family) of texts.

Codex Ephraemi (C) is a fifth century manuscript containing the entire New Testament except for 2 Thessalonians and 2 John. First published in 1845, it is called a *palimpsest*, which is a Greek word meaning 'rescraped', because someone tried to rub out the original text and write over the top of it. Fortunately, it is possible to discover the original, which is the New Testament text. The text is similar to *Codex Vaticanus*. *Ephraemi* is in the National Library of Paris.

Codex Bezae (D) was given to the University of Cambridge in 1581. It contains only the Gospels and Acts and part of 3 John and is clearly not very reliable in its text, since words and whole incidents are left out for no apparent reason. It is dated in the fifth or sixth centuries.

CURSIVES AND MINUSCULES

By the latter part of the first century, the large uncial (capital letters) of the Greek alphabet had been reduced to cursive, or joined-up writing; this enabled writing to be faster and smaller. Cursive was at first used for ordinary, everyday communication and often common words were abbreviated.

Cursives became attractive for those who wanted copies of the Scriptures both fast and cheap. The cost of professional copying would have been prohibitive for most Christian congregations. Late in the third century, the emperor Diocletian fixed the price of scribal work as a minimum of 20 denarii for 100 lines (*stichoi* as they were known). According to Matthew 20:2 a denarius would be the daily pay for a common labourer. On this basis, the Gospel of Luke would have cost around three months' wages for a professional scribe to copy. Some of the more literate church members doubtless copied for free.[37]

Inevitably care in transmission was sometimes more lax, and with the use of abbreviations and a running script, it was easy for a careless copier to slip here and there. However, with rare exceptions, these errors are small and easy to correct from the majority of texts available.

A development of the cursive style was the 'minuscule' writing which, as the word implies, meant that the letters were much smaller even than cursive. But this style was not adopted until sometime in the ninth century AD.

To date there are fifty-eight cursives of the complete New Testament, and thousands more of parts from fragments to almost whole books. In total, there are just over 2,800 cursives. Some go back to the third or fourth centuries, although most of this material comes between the ninth and fifteenth centuries. One, known as the 'Queen of the Cursives' is similar to *Codex Vaticanus*.

LECTIONARIES

Over two thousand lectionaries are available to us today. These were selected passages of Scripture used in worship, and their value is that they reveal the care with which they were copied; they can tell us what Greek text is being used, but they are not as old as the uncials.

THE VERSIONS

Just as there were versions (translations) of the Old Testament, so we have the same for the New Testament. The first evidence of a need to put the

---

37 See Bruce Metzger, *The Text of the New Testament*, pp. 15–16. William Barclay, *The Making of the Bible* (Lutterworth Press, London 1965), p. 46.

Greek text into another language comes from Africa as early as AD 180. Unfortunately, the versions are often translations from the Latin, and this does not help us to discover the Greek text. But a Syriac translation known as Tatian's *Diatessaron* is interesting since it may represent the text used by the Eastern church and is dated around AD 170. However, scholars are unsure whether it is based upon a Greek text.

Additionally, there are versions in Egyptian, Armenian, Georgian, Gothic, Ethiopian, Arabic, Syriac and many others. No great value can be placed upon some of these versions in the attempt to discover the best Greek text. One of the most famous versions is the Latin *Vulgate* of Jerome in the fourth century. Others, like the *Syriac Peshitta* from the fifth century, reveal more about content than texts; it does not include 2 Peter, 2 and 3 John, Jude or Revelation, which may indicate what books were still not fully accepted (or known?) in that area.

THE EARLY CHURCH LEADERS

Many of the early church leaders (generally referred to as 'Fathers') quote the New Testament in their writings, and from their references it is possible to discover what text they may have been using. We must bear in mind that these writers often quoted from memory or deliberately paraphrased. When they do this, we would not expect their quotations to agree, word for word, with any Greek text. Origen of Alexandria and Caesarea, who died in the mid-third century, rarely quoted a passage twice in precisely the same words. From Clement of Rome in AD 96 to Tertullian in AD 208 the church leaders were quoting the apostles and claiming authority for apostolic statements to challenge the heretics. Therefore, they must have held accurate and authentic copies, even if not the autographs themselves. There are so many quotations from the New Testament Scriptures in the writings of the early church leaders that it has been suggested we could reconstruct almost the whole New Testament if we had these writings alone.

From all that has been said, it is evident that scholars today have an immense amount of material available to help them discover the best Greek text. There are around five and a half thousand Greek manuscripts—

ranging from fragments of a few verses or even lines to the complete New Testament. This number includes 170 papyrus fragments, 2,754 minuscules and 266 uncials. In addition, there are thousands of versions and hundreds of quotations from early church leaders. It has been estimated that we have around 20,000 sources to help us piece together our New Testament.

It would be quite wrong to believe that this large quantity of material is a mass of confused and conflicting texts. The exact opposite is the case. In fact, by far the largest proportion of the New Testament finds full agreement in all the major sources, and nowhere does any Christian teaching depend upon an uncertain passage. However, there are differences, and where reliable texts differ from each other it is important to discover which text is most likely to reflect the original. Once again, a glance down the margin or at the foot of the page of a modern translation will show how comparatively few are the places where there is any significant doubt at all. See chapter 4 for more on the variations.

Some of the incomplete texts

THE *CHESTER BEATTY PAPYRI* (P45, P46)

Between 1930 and 1931, Chester Beatty, purchased some papyri which consisted of parts of the Old and New Testaments and the *Apocrypha*, the book of Enoch and a treatise by the second century leader, Melito of Sardis. Later, more sections were purchased. The most generally accepted date for this collection is AD 200 or at the latest 250.[38] P46 is possibly the oldest surviving collection of Paul's letters (ten in this case, including Hebrews). Originally dated around AD 200, in 1988 the palaeographer, Young-Kyu Kim, re-dated it to around AD 85.[39] The main objections to this early date are that it would be the oldest surviving Christian manuscript,

---

38 See Kurt Aland and Barbara Aland, *The Text of the New Testament*, Trans. E F Rhodes. (Eerdmans, Grand Rapids 1987), p. 99. Although Bruce Metzger, *The Text of the New Testament*, p. 38 opts for a date in the middle or late third century.
39 See Y-M Kim 'Paleographic Dating of P46 to the later First Century' in *Biblica*, 69 (1988), pp. 248–257. Quoted in *The Jesus Papyrus*, pp. 94,173. Bruce Metzger contradicts Kim in *The Text of the New Testament* (OUP 1992 third ed.), pp. 264–265.

the oldest surviving papyrus codex, the oldest use of abbreviations for the sacred names (known as *nomina sacra*). However, there is no reason, apart from assumptions, that it may not be all of these. The *Chester Beatty Papyri*, now in the Beatty Museum in Dublin, contain between them, fifteen books of the New Testament—clear evidence that by the middle of the third century significant collections of New Testament letters were already circulating.

THE *JOHN RYLANDS PAPYRUS* (P52)

The *John Rylands Papyrus* is housed in the John Rylands University Library in Manchester, England. Acquired in 1920 by the papyrologist B P Grenfell, it is a tiny fragment (6cm by 9cm) and contains only five verses from John 18:31–33, 37–38. It is part of a codex because vv. 37–38 are on the verso (reverse side). The fragment was dated around AD 125 by the papyrologist, Colin Roberts, Fellow of St John's College, Oxford, in 1935. Some two decades later he and Ramón Roca-Puig increased this to later in the second century. This was the latest possible date, and it meant that within one hundred years of John's death, a copy of his Gospel was already circulating in Egypt—a long way from where John wrote it in Ephesus.

The date of P52 is still a matter of discussion. Some scholars are convinced that it can be placed as far back as around the year AD 100.[40] In which case, to quote an earlier John Rylands Librarian: 'When the ink of the original autograph can hardly have been dry.'[41] Because of its clear similarities of style with P64 and P67 (see below), Carsten Thiede believes that P52 may be dated before AD 70.[42]

Bruce Metzger helpfully concludes that had this little fragment been known during the middle of the nineteenth century, the liberal critics from Germany like Ferdinand Baur 'could not have argued that the Fourth

---

40 See Bruce Metzger, *The Text of the New Testament*, p. 39 note 2.
41 Quote from H Guppy, *Transmission of the Bible* (1935), p. 4 in F F Bruce, *The Books and the Parchments* (Pickering & Inglis, London 1950), p. 172.
42 Thiede and D'Ancona, *The Jesus Papyrus* (Weidenfeld and Nicolson, London 1996), pp. 104–105.

Gospel was not composed until about the year 160'.[43] Unfortunately, many modern writers both of academic books and popular novels still seem to be unaware of this fact.

THE *BODMER PAPYRUS II* (P66)

Martin Bodmer acquired a valuable collection of papyri in Egypt in the 1950s. Among them is an almost complete codex of John's Gospel and is held by the Bodmer Library of World Literature at Cologny, Geneva, and known as the *Bodmer Papyrus II* (P66). It has generally been dated to AD 200, but more recently to c. AD 125.[44] If the latter, we have the text of John's Gospel within possibly thirty years of his death. There are many alterations and corrections in P66 which implies that it was copied in haste—the probable reason why it was discarded and thus preserved.

THE *BODMER PAPYRUS* (P75)

Dated between AD 175 and 225 it contains almost the whole of Luke and John and is therefore the earliest example of an (almost) complete copy of Luke's Gospel, and one of the earliest of John. Also in the Bodmer Library, 102 pages of 144 have survived, and it is in carefully written uncial letters. It is more evidence of the circulation of the Gospels before the close of the second century.

Other documents in this collection include portions of 1 and 2 Peter and Jude, Acts and Paul's epistles, but these are dated later in the third and fourth centuries.

There are many more codices, but as they become progressively later in date, for many scholars they are less of interest to discover the best text. There are ongoing debates over whether these codices have been preserved because of their accuracy or simply because they were not used as they were unreliable. However, the one thing that we can affirm is that early in the fourth century complete sets of the Bible, as well as separate collections of New Testament books, were circulating among the churches.

---

43 Bruce Metzger, *The Text of the New Testament*, p. 39.
44 As above, *The Jesus Papyrus*, p. 124 and see on the work of Herbert Hunger p. 174 note 2. Also Metzger, *The Text of the New Testament*, p. 40 note 1.

Papyrology and a few significant fragments

This next section is presented in some detail for those who like a little detective work! It is of interest in evidencing an early date for the individual books. We are dealing here with very small fragments of text, but they are not unimportant.

The science of papyrology is the highly skilled task of taking a small sample of ancient parchment and identifying what it is: its place of origin, its date and, even more important, what piece of literature it represents. Sometimes the papyrologist is working with a tiny fragment of a few words, some indecipherable or broken, over just a few lines. It may seem an impossible task, but not for the worker skilled in languages and ancient documents.

A simple illustration will show how possible it is to identify the book from which a small fragment is taken. If you were to rip out a page from this book you are reading, then tear a one inch diameter section at random from any part of that page, you would be left with approximately fifty letters, or parts of letters, over five lines—and perhaps some on the reverse side as well. It would be possible to reconstruct most of the incomplete letters by your knowledge of the English language, though this would not complete all the words for you. The 'predictive text' on a modern phone and 'auto correction' on a computer illustrate how extremely accurate this can be. Surprising though it may seem, having got this far, and given such factors as font size, type face and spacing, it is virtually impossible that your small fragment would fit any other book in existence other than this particular publication. It may take you some time to narrow down your search to this book, but once found, your identification could be exact. That is what the science of papyrology is about.

In what follows, we will trace the intriguing story of some of the oldest fragments of the New Testament. For our purpose, it does not matter that they are only fragments—it is their existence and their date that matters. For example, if it could be proven without any doubt, that a fragment of one of the Gospels had been discovered and dated well before the end of the first century, say at around AD 68, then it would be proven without question that that Gospel, or a significant part of it, was in existence at that time—and that the original must have been written earlier. We do not need to find the complete document to arrive at this conclusion.

Again, to use an illustration: Many books published in the nineteenth century did not carry a date of publication, and at times this is most frustrating for researchers. However, if the researcher discovers a dated letter in which the writer quotes from that book, or better still a fragment of one of the pages which, by the context of where it was found, can be accurately dated, then at least he can affirm that the book itself was written sometime prior to that known date. That is what papyrologists, with the aid of other specialists, aim to do.

Radio carbon dating is of little use to the papyrologists concerned with the texts that follow. In the first place, that method can only be accurate to plus or minus fifty years, and that is too wide a margin of error for our purposes. Secondly, the method demands the destruction of the material offered for sample, and whilst this is only a few grams, it would often mean the loss of vital letters, or even spaces, from the original. Dating is therefore mainly by the type of ink and parchment or papyrus used, the handwriting and known characteristics of style—in much the same way that a modern forensic handwriting expert would operate—and of course any artefacts that are found in the same location.

We are now ready to look at a few of the earliest known 'scraps' of the New Testament. When Sir Frederick Kenyon, Director of the British Museum, wrote in 1936 that the *Chester Beatty Papyri* were 'the earliest copies of the Bible as yet known to exist',[45] he little knew what lay only a few years ahead.

In 1996 a storm of scholarly debate was aroused by the publication of *The Jesus Papyrus*. In this book Carsten Thiede, working in Germany as a recognised expert in the field of dating early writing, dated three fragments of papyrus held in the library at Magdalen College, Oxford. They had been identified as part of Matthew 26 and Thiede asserted that they were written some years before the fall of Jerusalem in AD 70. The

---

45 Sir Frederick Kenyon, *The Story of the Bible* (John Murray, London 1949), p. 14.

book quickly became a best-seller, spawned a TV documentary and raised strong discussion with experts lining up to agree or disagree. The case may not be proved, but if it is, it is yet another indication that those who insist on a third century date (or later) for the writing of the Gospels, would be wise to think again.

QUMRAN FRAGMENT (7Q5)—A FRAGMENT FROM MARK'S GOSPEL?

Among the fragments that had been found from 1947 onwards in the caves around the Dead Sea, one lay unidentified for years in the Rockefeller Museum in Jerusalem. Whilst checking the catalogue of biblical manuscripts in the Vatican Library in Rome, Jose O'Callaghan found himself intrigued by a small text discovered in cave 7 at Qumran as late as 1955 and labelled simply as 'Fragment not identified. 7Q5'. Cave 7 was separate from the other Qumran caves and much closer to Jericho.

Among his many qualifications, Father Jose O'Callaghan was Professor of Greek Papyrology and Palaeography at the Pontifical Biblical Institute in Rome, and he has been described as 'An accomplished papyrologist whose previous publications have been characterised by scholarly insight and balanced judgement.'[46] O'Callaghan had long been recognised as a leading scholar in his field and he studied the original 7Q5 document in the Rockefeller Museum.

7Q5 was part of eighteen fragments all written in Greek (not Aramaic) and on papyrus (not parchment) that were discovered scattered on the floor of the cave; it was also part of a scroll not a codex, since the writing was on one side of the papyrus only, and it was in a clearly identifiable 'decorative' capital (uncial) script. All this was important information. The 7Q5 fragment contained only nineteen letters, half of them incomplete, on just five lines.

That may not sound much, but a papyrologist of O'Callaghan's experience was used to working with far less than this. The same cave had revealed twenty-two letters on five lines that had been confidently

---

46 Bruce Metzger, quoted in Estrada and White, *The First New Testament* (Thomas Nelson Inc., New York 1978), p. 79 but not referenced.

identified as part of an apocryphal book Baruch 6:43-44. By comparison, the oldest known papyrus fragment of Virgil, discovered at Masada in 1989, contains fifteen letters (two of which are almost illegible) on one line, and these have been reliably identified as *Aeneid* 4:9—and no one questions this. So, this small fragment is well within the workspace of an experienced papyrologist.

Jose O'Callaghan focused on four letters: *nnes*, and eventually concluded that they must be part of the word Gennesaret. No other known Greek word would fit. That could have come from 1 Maccabees 11:67 in the *Apocrypha*, but the rest of the text simply would not fit that verse. This drew him to the same word found in the New Testament Gospel of Mark. The whole fragment neatly fitted the space required for Mark 6:52-53, 'for they had not understood about the loaves; their hearts were hardened. When they had crossed over, they landed at Gennesaret and anchored there.' There was even a blank space, the length of almost three letters, at the end of our verse 52, which was a known way of indicating a break long before verse numbers had been added.

What made this discovery even more challenging was the fact that the contents of cave 7 had already been fixed as having been deposited no later than AD 68 and there is no evidence that it was ever reopened until archaeologists discovered the cave in 1955. Suggestions have been made that perhaps Christians revisited the cave after that date and then deposited the text, but this is a forlorn hope dismissed by all archaeologists. Carsten Thiede, whose work on another text (P64) we will consider below, has commented: 'All serious archaeological investigation has discounted the idea that ... the Qumran caves were re-inhabited after AD 68.'[47]

---

47 Thiede and D'Ancona, *The Jesus Papyrus* (Weidenfeld and Nicolson, London 1996), p.55. Note that the defence by Thiede and D'Ancona of the general conclusions of O'Callaghan were after the intervention of more than two decades of debate on the subject; there can be little more information to come to light. Detractors have had their opportunity. Strangely, in a generally useful book, *Archaeology and the New Testament* (Baker Book House, Michigan 1991), John McRay spends only twelve lines on the fragments of Qumran 7 and casually dismisses them as 'too scanty for positive identification'; he makes no mention of the scholarly confirmation by Thiede or Estrada, even though the latest edition of his book in 2001 postdates their work.

More than this, long before O'Callaghan had identified the text, experts had dated the actual writing as no later than the end of the first century.[48] In fact, the same decorative uncial script—though in copies of pagan philosophers -- has been found in the remains of Herculaneum in Italy which was covered in volcanic ash by Mount Vesuvius in AD 79. The conclusion is simple: These fragments from the Dead Sea cave 7 are evidence of manuscripts of the Christian New Testament, written in neat decorative script, before AD 68.[49] And since these are assumed to be copies and not by the hand of the original writers, the autographs must go back even earlier.

O'Callaghan published his work in many journals and, as would be expected when a very early New Testament text is found, there were many who opposed his conclusions.[50] Generally, it should be noted, the opposition came from New Testament critical scholars and theologians and not from the scientists. Someone was quick to point out the relevance of part of the text of Mark 6:52, 'they had not understood … their hearts were hardened'!

In 1994 'one of the greatest papyrologists of our time', Orsolina Montevecchi, then Honorary President of the International Papyrologists Association, concluded: 'I do not think that there can be any doubt about the identification of 7Q5.'[51]

After years of debate, no satisfactory alternative explanation has been offered for the existence of a text from the Gospel of Mark in a cave whose contents were sealed by AD 68, and in which there is no evidence of later

---

48 By the respected British scholar Colin H Roberts. Though it has to be said that Roberts dismissed O'Callaghan's identification of the text as 'an exercise not in scholarship but in fantasy'. See, *The First New Testament*, p. 27. Was this a churlish response by one scholar who failed to identify the text where another succeeded?
49 Estrada and White, *The First New Testament*, p. 123. See especially their conclusions on pp. 126–131.
50 See particularly, *Los papiros Griegos de la Cueva 7 de Qumran* (Madrid 1974). But a detailed discussion of his results in English will be found in Estrada and White, *The First New Testament*. On the other hand, Bruce Metzger in *The Text of the New Testament* (OUP 1992 third ed), pp. 264-5, disputed O'Callaghan's identification as merely 'interesting coincidences', though Thiede, Estrada and others have answered all his objections.
51 *The Jesus Papyrus*, p. 56.

intrusion. Had the conclusions run the other way, they would have been accepted without question, but because all the known evidence to date points to the completion *and copying* of the Gospel of Mark, or at least part of it, well before the fall of Jerusalem in AD 70, it must be resisted at all costs.

FROM THE SAME CAVE 7Q4—A FRAGMENT FROM 1 TIMOTHY?

O'Callaghan claims that nine other fragments from the same cave fit perfectly parts of the New Testament, especially 1 Timothy 3:16, 4:1-3 (7Q4); Mark 4:28 (7Q6); and James 1:23,24 (7Q8).[52] The suggestion that 1 Timothy and James could be found in texts dating before AD 68 is a conclusion that John Wenham sympathetically admits, 'is almost too shocking to be contemplated!'[53]

Significantly, the most vigorous arguments against this identification from 1 Timothy comes from those who do not believe that Paul wrote the letter to Timothy. However, the strength of 7Q4 on these verses in Timothy is that it contains the end of five lines, which makes it far easier to identify—try discovering more than one piece of literature with five consecutive lines that close with identical words, all copied before AD 68. The odds against this are astronomical.

Whether O'Callaghan is correct in every case, the portions referred to above, and not least 7Q5 and 7Q4, are virtually certain. No other identifications have been offered for these fragments, and if it were not for the fact that they are incredibly early evidence of portions of the Gospels and letters of Paul, there would be little debate about most of them.

The evidence is that well before the destruction of Herculaneum in AD 79, or of Jerusalem in AD 70, Christians were using copies of their sacred texts—the Gospels and the letters of Paul for example—from the best decorative scripts possible.

In 1846 the German liberal critic of the Bible, D F Strauss, suggested that 'It would be an argument of decisive weight in favour of the credibility

---

52 For a more cautious, though positive treatment, see *The Jesus Papyrus*, pp. 125–126
53 John Wenham, *Redating Matthew, Mark and Luke* (Hodder & Stoughton, London 1991), p. 179.

of the biblical history, could it indeed be shown that it was written by eye-witnesses or even by persons nearly contemporaneous with the events narrated.'[54] Here, then, is the first part of that evidence. After the publication of O'Callaghan's work, *Time* magazine commented that it was now time 'To make a bonfire of seventy tons of indigestible German scholarship.'

THE *MAGDALEN FRAGMENT* P64—A FRAGMENT FROM MATTHEW'S GOSPEL?

This story concerns three small scraps of parchment belonging to Magdalen College in Oxford. The largest, identified by Carsten Thiede, Director of the Institute for Basic Epistemological Research in Paderborn, Germany, contained fragments of Matthew 26. The text that Thiede was working on had been discovered in Upper Egypt by the Rev. Charles Bousfield Huleatt in 1901. Shortly before the tragic death of him and his family in an earthquake at Messinesi on 28 December 1908, Huleatt sent these fragments of an ancient text to his alma mater at Magdalen College, where they were duly filed as 'P. Magdalen Greek 17/P64' and remained unidentified for almost half a century.[55]

The papyrologist, Colin Roberts, had worked on these texts in the 1950s and published his work 'An Early Papyrus of the First Gospel' in 1953 in the Harvard Theological Review.[56] He noted that the largest was only 4.1 cm by 1.3 cm. On this fragment there would have been 15 or 16 letters to a line and it was written in double column to a page, and was probably bound into a book on its own that would have amounted to some 150 pages. The fragments, written on both sides of the page, contain parts of Matthew 28:7–8, 10 ,14–15, 22–23, 31–33. The largest section contained thirty-seven letters (or parts of letters) over four lines. Roberts dated the fragments as late in the second century, which made them at least the oldest known texts of Matthew's Gospel.

---

54 D F Strauss, *The Life of Jesus*, translated from the German (Chapman, London 1846), Vol. 1, p. 88.

55 His story is told in detail, together with the account of the identification of these P64 fragments in Thiede and D'Ancona, *The Jesus Papyrus*.

56 *Harvard Theological Review*, 1953, no. 46, pp. 233–237.

Carsten Thiede undertook detailed and careful research on the fragments and came to a different conclusion from Roberts on the date. The fact that P64 is part of a codex rather than a scroll does not at all preclude a much earlier date for it. The Italian papyrologist, Italo Gallo, has shown that the codex was in common use by Christians 'not later than 70 AD'.[57] This is now generally accepted. Similarly, the form of writing in the *Magdalen fragment*—Greek capitals (uncial)—is virtually identical to the writing of a fragment also discovered in Egypt, though not a biblical text, that dates itself as the twelfth year of the Emperor Nero, which is AD 66.[58] Similarly, the presence of shorthand forms for the divine names in the text (*nomina sacra*) is known to have been used before the turn of the first century; the handwriting used in the Magdalen fragments is similar to other texts dated in that century.

Thiede dated these fragments to sometime before AD 70, and commented on the early date of this fragment of Matthew's Gospel:

'This is an unpalatable conclusion for New Testament scholars convinced that St Matthews' Gospel is a later, community creation, describing Jesus … in a way which would meet the liturgical needs of the eighties of the first century. To some academics and many ordinary Christians however, already convinced that the Gospels consist of authentic eyewitness material from apostolic times, the result had come as no surprise.'[59]

This perceptive comment perhaps shows why many theologians and New Testament scholars have been so reluctant to accept, or even engage with, the results of Thiede's careful work—presuppositions are hard to abandon. If Thiede is correct, it means that the full text from which P64 is a small part, could have been copied in the lifetime of Matthew himself. Thiede comments that, 'The instinct to undermine the Gospels has overtaken the pre-modern instinct to take their truth for granted …

---

57 I Gallo, *Greek and Latin Papyrology* (London 1986), p. 14. Quoted by Thiede, *The Jesus Papyrus*, p. 106.
58 Thiede and D'Ancona, *The Jesus Papyrus*, pp. 111–112.
59 *The Jesus Papyrus*, p. 112.

Some scholars and writers will go to almost any length to avoid the charge of credulity.'[60]

John A T Robinson, a contemporary liberal critic, similarly admitted to: 'The consistent evasion by modern commentators of a solution they have already prejudged to be impossible.'[61]

THE *BARCELONA PAPYRI* P67—MORE FROM MATTHEW'S GOSPEL

Housed at the Fundación San Lucas Evangelista, in Barcelona,[62] the Barcelona Papyri consist of two fragments containing parts of Matthew 3:9,15 and 5:20–22,25–28 and are clearly part of a codex because they are written on both sides.

The papyrologist Colin Roberts accepted that both P67 and P64 were most likely written by the same hand (though probably not part of the same codex) and this has since been confirmed independently by Carsten Thiede and Philip Comfort.[63] Because of their uncial style, Roberts dated them to the second century. However, this careful scribal style pre-dates the first century and this means that the once generally accepted date of early second century might now be revised to well before the close of the previous century.

THE *PARIS PAPYRUS* P4—SOMETHING FROM LUKE'S GOSPEL?

This papyrus, held at the Bibliothèque Nationale in Paris, is larger than both the *Magdalen* (P64) and *Barcelona* (P67) fragments and contains large parts of Luke 1–6. It is not linked with the other two, though may have come from the same scribal school and only a little later in date. Thiede dates it as around AD 70 whilst Comfort is more cautious at early in the second century.[64] What is virtually certain, therefore, is that we have a significant portion of Luke's Gospel circulating in neat uncial format early in the second century at the latest.

---

60 *The Jesus Papyrus*, p. 135.
61 John A T Robinson, *Redating the New Testament* (SCM Press, London 1976), p. 342.
62 In the Gregory-Aland list of New Testament papyri.
63 *The Jesus Papyrus*, p. 89.
64 As above, pp. 89-91.

AROUND THE CORNER?

There are many more odds and ends that could be described: P77 is a small papyrus fragment from a codex of Matthew 23:30–39, originally dated late second century, then AD 150, but it could be much older. P1 resides in the University of Pennsylvania and is a good example of Matthew 1:1–9, 12, 14–20, which may be not much older than the Magdalen fragments.

However, much more may yet come to light. There are many unopened and yet uncovered scrolls at Herculaneum, the city devastated by Vesuvius in AD 79. There was most likely a Christian community here, so what texts may they have been using? Whilst the arguments in favour of an early date for any one of these fragments may be disputed—and certainly will be by critics because too much swings on the evidence—the cumulative data is a powerful argument for the circulation of copies of the New Testament records well before the close of the first century.

4. Discovering the best text

It is pious dreaming to imagine that all our Bible translations are based upon a single, undisputed text that exactly corresponds to the very words penned by the prophets and apostles. We must work at finding the best text.

I n the previous two chapters we introduced the huge amount of material that is available for the early texts of the Bible. Since we have no manuscripts actually written by a prophet or apostle (the autographs), in their search for an accurate text for the Old and New Testaments scholars must sort through the many copies. This is called 'textual criticism'. It is a detailed and exacting science, and the results take time and patience. What follows here is only a glance at a complex issue. However, the serious reader of the Bible should not be intimidated by the subject.

The text of the Old Testament

Compared with the New Testament, there is far less complexity in discovering the best text for the Old. The main reason for this is that there is considerably less material available. In chapter 2, we surveyed some of the Hebrew manuscripts and versions with which scholars can work. For simplicity, we may define those of significance as: the *Masoretic Text* (Hebrew), the *Septuagint* (Greek), and the *Dead Sea Scrolls* (Hebrew). We have already noted the extreme care of the Masoretes in the ninth century, and they followed a long tradition of such detailed attention for the accurate copying of the sacred texts. For this reason, the *Masoretic Text*, which is the basis for all our English translations, is certainly the best. Few scholars would disagree with this.

However, there are occasions where the translators may not be certain of the meaning of a Hebrew word and here the *Septuagint* may help since it was a translation in the third century BC into Greek from a Hebrew text. In the book of Job, generally considered to be one of the earliest of our Old Testament books, the translators of the *English Standard Version* admit that there are at least fifteen places (and one whole section in 34:29–33) where the meaning of the Hebrew words is uncertain; when Tyndale was translating Job in the early sixteenth century he was faced with an even larger area of uncertainty because Hebrew was less well-known then. However, we noted earlier that the *Septuagint* is not always reliable and therefore translators will only cautiously use it in preference to the *Masoretic Text*.

The *Septuagint* was not always wrong, and a simple illustration of this is found in the text of Hebrews 11:21. Here, Jacob is said to have blessed Joseph's two sons 'as he leaned on the top of his staff.' Although the writer is not claiming to quote from the Old Testament, in Genesis 47:31 the Hebrew *Masoretic Text* informs us that Jacob 'bowed down at the head of his bed'. We noted in chapter 2 that until the time of the Masoretes (after AD 600), the Hebrew was written without vowels. The Hebrew word for 'bed' has just three consonants in it, MTH, and the Hebrew word for 'staff' has the same three consonants, MTH. Therefore, the Masoretes could have rendered the same word either by 'bed' or 'staff'; the difference meant the addition of the vowel, 'i' or 'a'. The Masoretes chose the word 'bed' and assumed the vowel was 'i', whilst the translators of the *Septuagint*, working long before the Masoretes, chose the word 'staff' and assumed the vowel was 'a'. But which is right? The most straightforward conclusion is that since the word used in Genesis 47 could be either 'bed' or 'staff' the Masoretes made an error of judgement in their choice, and the New Testament writer, directed by the Holy Spirit (1 Corinthians 2:13), gives us the correct translation in Hebrews 11:21. Whilst Genesis 47:31 was inspired by the Spirit (so the consonants are right), the Masoretes were not (therefore the vowels may be wrong).

At other times the *Septuagint* may fill a gap or try to help where the Hebrew is a little obscure. In Genesis 2:2 the Hebrew text literally reads 'On the seventh day God finished the work he had been doing.' Since this seventh day was to be a pattern of rest for Israel, it is obvious to almost all readers that it meant God had finished his work *before* the seventh day. However, some may consider it confusing so, lest there be any misunderstanding, the *Septuagint*, the *Samaritan Pentateuch* and the Syriac *Peshitta*, all read 'On the sixth day God finished his work…' An unnecessary change.

On the other hand, Genesis 4:8 reads: 'Now Cain said to his brother Abel, "Let's go out to the field"' (*New International Version*). The *Masoretic Text* reads simply: 'And Cain said to his brother Abel.' Clearly, something is missing, and some translations render it: 'And Cain told (or spoke to) Abel his brother' (The *King James Version*, *Revised Version* and *New American Standard Bible*, *English Standard Version*); however, this involves changing the Hebrew verb. The *Septuagint* translation may have used a Hebrew text that included the words: 'Let's go out into the field' (or it may simply have added them) and therefore some translations, like the NIV, have followed the *Septuagint* here.

Far less helpfully, we noted in chapter 2 a text of the *Septuagint* which apparently added the words *'from the tree'* to Psalm 96:10 to make it a Messianic promise: 'Say among the nations, "The LORD reigns *from the tree*."' Clearly a later addition by an over-zealous Christian copyist.

The accuracy of the work of the Masoretes is illustrated by the agreed fact that their text was clearly the same as that used by Jewish writings and the early church leaders (Origen's *Hexapla* for example), centuries before the Masoretes began their work—as far back as the second century.[65] The close agreement with the *Masoretic Text* of both the *Septuagint* and the Dead Sea texts is also witness to the accuracy of the Hebrew Old Testament.

In the previous chapter the significance of the *Dead Sea Scrolls* was outlined. What is particularly important is the fact that the Dead Sea copy of Isaiah is remarkably in line with the earliest *Masoretic Text*. There are differences, but they are few and most are insignificant.[66] Some

---

65 Karen Jobes and Moisés Silva, *Invitation to the Septuagint* (Baker Academic, Grand Rapids, Michigan, 2000), p. 147.

66 We should be aware of those who suggest there are tens of thousands of differences between the Dead Sea Scrolls and the Masoretic Text – they are referring to the differences of grammar, spelling, punctuation and the like. These are not errors and rarely change the meaning of the text.

scholars will only allow four occasions where the Dead Sea text of Isaiah is different from and better than the *Masoretic Text*. The differences are overwhelmingly confined to words or even letters. Here is just one typical example: The *Masoretic Text* for Isaiah 40:12 reads, 'Who has measured the waters [Hebrew *mayim*] in the hollow of his hand?' whereas the Dead Sea text reads, 'Who has measured the waters of the sea [Hebrew *mê yam*] in the hollow of his hand?' Such a scribal difference is easily understood and changes nothing of the meaning.

One Dead Sea text of Isaiah was available in time for the team working on the *Revised Standard Version* in 1952 to make use of it. From the entire scroll, the translation team adopted only thirteen readings from the Dead Sea text in preference to the *Masoretic Text*. One of the leading team members later regretted the adoption of some of these thirteen.

The *New International Version* of 1984 lists no more than sixteen occasions in Isaiah where it sees any need even to note that the Dead Sea text and the *Masoretic Text* differ; on eleven of these occasions the Dead Sea text is preferred, but sometimes only because the Masoretic word is unclear. Here are the first few such notes, the rest are similar in importance: in 7:14 Dead Sea has 'and he' or 'and they' instead of the Masoretic 'and'. In 14:4 the translators adopt the Dead Sea, 'fury' because the meaning of the Masoretic word is unclear. 15:9 is a matter of spelling a name either *Dimon* (*Masoretic Text*) or *Dibon* (Dead Sea). In 19:18 most Masoretic texts have 'City of Destruction' whereas Dead Sea has 'City of the Sun'. Some of the *Dead Sea Scrolls* of Old Testament books are closer to the *Septuagint* than to the *Masoretic Text*, but even then, the similarities are remarkable and differences are chiefly of the order noted above—occasional words and spelling.

The English Standard Version (2001/8) allows only nine places where the translators preferred the Dead Sea text of Isaiah over the *Masoretic Text* (14:4; 15:9; 21:8; 40:6; 49:12,17,24, 25; 51:19). These variances are all a matter of a word or short phrase or where the meaning of the Hebrew of the *Masoretic Text* is uncertain, as in 14:4. In 15:9 'Dibon' is chosen from the *Dead Sea Scrolls* in preference to 'Dimon' in the *Masoretic Text*. In 21:8 'then he who saw it cried out', in preference to 'then he cried out like a lion'. In 40:6 'a voice says', in preference to 'and someone says'. In 49:12 'Syene', in preference to 'Sinim'. In 49:17 'you builders make haste', in preference to 'your children make haste'. In 49:24,25, 'captives of a tyrant', in place of 'captives of a righteous man'. In 51:19 'who will comfort you', in place of 'how shall I comfort you?' This amounts to nine small changes in nine verses out of 1,286 verses in our English Bible of Isaiah. This does not mean these are the only differences between the two, but the only occasion when the translators considered the *Dead Sea Scrolls* offered a better reading. In addition, they noted five occasions where they chose to ignore the Dead Sea variant and six where they chose to ignore the *Septuagint* variant.

It is therefore evident that the Hebrew text underlying the Old Testament has a long history of accurate copying and that where there are differences between various Greek and Hebrew texts, they are mostly confined to words or phrases which make little, if any, difference to the meaning of the Scripture.

The widespread use of the *Septuagint* by the writers of the New Testament letters has been discussed also in Book 2 chapter 4 in this series under, 'How the apostles "quoted" from the Old Testament'.

The text of the New Testament

From all that we have seen in the previous chapter, it is evident that copies of the New Testament books were circulating among the churches before the close of the first century. To take just one example, Clement of Rome wrote to the church at Corinth around AD 95 and invited them:

'Take up the epistle of the blessed Apostle Paul. What did he write to you at the time when the Gospel first began to be preached? Truly, under the inspiration of the Spirit, he wrote to you concerning himself, and Cephas, and Apollos, because even then parties had been formed among you...'[67]

Clement could assume that the church at Corinth still held a copy of Paul's letters to them.

---

67 1 Clement 47.

Evidently, the churches were eager to obtain and copy the books that were from apostolic authorship. Naturally copies meant that occasional mistakes crept in. However, we should remind ourselves that B F Westcott, whose skill as a New Testament textual critic is still recognised after one hundred and fifty years, claimed that 'substantial variation' between the texts can hardly form more than a 'thousandth part' of the whole New Testament,[68] and the acclaimed biblical scholar F F Bruce concluded, 'There is no body of ancient literature in the world which enjoys such a wealth of good textual attestation as the New Testament.'[69]

Because there is so much material available for our New Testament text, and because there are some differences between them, it is the task of the textual critic, to discover the best text. In 1796 Johann Jakob Griesbach, Professor of New Testament at the University of Jena in Germany, set out fifteen 'rules' for deciding on the best text. He also classified the available New Testament documents into three 'families', and this is generally followed today. See the previous chapter for the texts referred to below; these are the main representatives of each group:

First, those that come from the Byzantine (Syrian) Empire, the Eastern part of the Roman Empire, which was based upon Constantinople and lasted from the fourth century and continued with steadily declining power until 1453 when the Turks captured that city. This includes the *Majority Text*.

Second, those that reflect a Western origin with Rome as the centre. This includes *Bezae*.

Third, those that reflect an Eastern source, with Alexandria as the centre. *Sinaiticus, Vaticanus, Ephraemi*.

However, the division is not as neat and simple as this implies.

Griesbach was the first scholar seriously to challenge the Byzantine text (see the *Received Text* below) as the only permitted text for New

---

68 Westcott, *The New Testament in the Original Greek*, p. 2.
69 F F Bruce, *The Books and the Parchments* (Pickering & Inglis, London 1950), p. 170.

Testament translation. His first edition of the text was published in 1775 and he was followed shortly after by another German scholar, Karl Lachmann. However, Lachman did not propose a definitive Greek text because he limited himself to Greek texts and versions and the writing of the church Fathers to the end of the fourth century. To search for an original text from the references to Scripture in the writing of the early church Fathers would be somewhat like attempting to identify a particular translation from the free quotations and paraphrases of a selection of modern preachers. However, as we will see, it was Tischendorf who later brought the subject into a modern focus.

It is the task of the textual critic to compare the various 'families' or groups of texts to discover the best reading wherever there may be a difference among available texts.

Since the first edition of Erasmus in 1516 and Estienne's *Received Text* in 1550, there have been any number of attempts to compile a definitive text of the Greek New Testament with which everyone would agree.[70] In order to simplify the problem we can divide the approach into the three groups.

THE *RECEIVED TEXT*

It is the conviction of many Christians that since God gave a verbally infallible Scripture, he must have protected a pure Greek text upon which the church could later base all translations. There is no clear biblical argument in favour of this view since the Scripture insistence on its own revelation from God refers to the autographs; future copies and translations were not in focus. Therefore, we should beware of making this view a matter of essential belief.

This text is known as the *Received Text* or *Textus Receptus*. (See the previous chapter under, The New Testament manuscripts.) This title was not used until 1633, but it did refer to a Greek text that had become standard for all translations across Europe and was basically the text of

---

70 For a detailed discussion of the history of the New Testament text see Bruce M Metzger, *The Text of the New Testament* (OUP, New York and Oxford 1992). Metzger, like all scholars, was not wholly unbiased in his preferences.

Stephanus (Estienne) of 1550 which was close to Erasmus' final edition in 1527. Bishop Ellicott, the chairman of the committee that produced the Greek text for the *Revised Version*, commented, 'The manuscripts which Erasmus used differ, for the most part, only in small and insignificant details from the great bulk of the cursive manuscripts.[71] The general character of their text is the same.' Ellicott continued that the ancestors of the texts used for the *Received Text* must go back as far as, possibly much further than, any of our existing texts. This is a good recommendation and there is no reason why we should not treat the *Received Text* with great respect.

The *Received Text* comes from the Byzantine (Syrian) family of texts. It is sometimes referred to as the *Majority Text* because more than eighty per cent of our Greek texts belong to it. There are minor differences between these texts but their overwhelming agreement is significant. However, since these texts are dated to the ninth century, and some believe they all come from a fourth century revision by Lucianus, it is assumed they are all copies from the same early text and therefore their value is not decided merely by counting the numbers. Although the idea of a revision by Lucianus is a theory with no factual support, the *Majority Text* is clearly a copy of much earlier texts. From the fact that the majority of our Greek texts come from this family it can be argued that it was the most widely used text for the New Testament among the early churches.

There are some difficulties in accepting the *Received Text* as the only text from which we should work. First, Estienne's text of 1550 was not the only text to be called the *Received Text*. In fact, it was a text of two Dutch brothers by the name of Elzevir that first called itself *Textum Receptum*, but this edition was not published until 1633 and therefore was too late for the translators of the *King James Version* who had completed their work by 1611. There were many New Testament Greek texts produced between 1516 and 1524, all with minor differences and each using more Greek manuscripts than the one before it. Any one of them could have

---

71 Cursive writing was the Greek joined-up form of writing developed in the first century AD. See the previous chapter under, New Testament manuscripts.

been chosen as the *Received Text*. Besides this, in places (for example, Acts 8:37; 1 John 5:7–8; Revelation 22:16–21) the text produced by Erasmus does not follow any Byzantine Text, but the Latin *Vulgate*.

The second problem is that a few complete texts of the Greek New Testament, such as *Sinaiticus*, *Vaticanus* and *Alexandrinus* which are dated to the fourth century, and thousands of fragments even older than these and none of which were known to Erasmus have come to light since 1550. What are we to do with them? To ignore them all would seem both unscholarly and against reason; to claim that they have been preserved for so long because they were unreliable and therefore unused is an argument that could dispense with all the *Dead Sea Scrolls* also. We can hardly claim that God preserved these other texts in order to test our faith in the *Received Text*. So, why do we have them if we should not use them?

A third problem with the *Received Text*, is that there are some very definite weaknesses in Estienne's text. When Erasmus' Greek texts ended at Revelation 22:16 he simply retranslated the Latin *Vulgate* back to Greek. In Revelation 22:19 Erasmus, using the *Vulgate*, translated into Greek 'God will take away from him his share in the book of life.' All Greek manuscripts available today read 'tree of life'—the reading we would expect from the context. One scholar in his detailed defence of the *Received Text* claims of this: 'Here he (Erasmus) may have been guided providentially by the common faith to follow the Latin *Vulgate*.'[72] In reality it would appear that Erasmus was translating from a Latin text in which a careless scribe had read the correct word *ligno* ('tree') as *libro* ('book'). This one word change is not of great importance, but it does reveal a problem in suggesting that the *Received Text* is a perfect Greek text.

Possibly of more significance is the question of 1 John 5:7 'For there are three who bear witness in heaven: The Father, the Word and the Holy Spirit; and these three are one.' This is known as the *Comma Johanneum*. Erasmus found it in the Latin *Vulgate*, but in no Greek manuscript; he therefore omitted it from his Greek text in 1516. The outcry was so

---

72 E F Hills, *The King James Version Defended*. On-line download, p.161. Also available from Christian Research Press (1997).

great that he declared if one Greek manuscript could be produced which included this verse, he too would include it. Conveniently, a manuscript was produced, and in his 3rd edition in 1522, Erasmus placed it in his text but with a note declaring his suspicion that it had been written for the occasion. That single manuscript is now in the library of Trinity College, Dublin and is widely believed to have been written around the year 1520.[73] We cannot attribute its presence to Jerome since the earliest evidence of it is in a Latin *Vulgate* of AD 800—four centuries after Jerome.

There is some possible evidence for the early appearance of 1 John 5:7 because Cyprian of Carthage may have alluded to this text around the year AD 250. However, it is more likely to have been an early Christian statement of Trinitarian belief that eventually found its way into the Latin texts. The only defence for its presence in the *Received Text* is the suggestion that it, 'Somehow dropped out of the Greek New Testament but was preserved in the Latin text through the usage of the Latin speaking church,'[74] and that this verse is therefore 'possibly genuine'.[75] No adequate explanation can be offered as to why such an important statement would 'drop out' of the Greek text, and 'possibly genuine' does not bring us to certainty. The opinion of Martin Luther is well known when he offered two hundred florins to anyone who could produce just one Greek text with it in adding, with his florins in mind, 'God alone knows where I will find them.'

What is undisputed, however, is that this particular verse has never been part of the *Majority Text* even though it was added later to the *Received Text*. To accept 1 John 5:7 is to accept the later *Received Text* of 1522 and ignore the *Majority Text*. The Christian doctrine of the Trinity does not depend upon this single verse.

Two other passages, that are found in the *Received Text* although not in many Greek manuscripts discovered more recently—Mark 16:9–20 and John 7:53 to 8:11—will be discussed later in this chapter.

---

73 For example, C H Turner, *The Early Printed Editions of the Greek New Testament* (OUP, Oxford 1924), pp. 23-24. Referenced in Metzger, *The Text of the New Testament*, p. 101.
74 E F Hills, above, p. 169.
75 E F Hills, above, p. 167.

THE TEXT OF WESTCOTT AND HORT

Griesbach was the first to move away from the *Received Text* when he felt the evidence pointed favourably in the direction of a variant text. Others soon followed. In 1831 Karl Lachmann published a Greek text in which he abandoned all the minuscules that lay behind the *Received Text* and struck out on his own. But it was Tischendorf, who had discovered the codex *Sinaiticus* (see the previous chapter), who laid a foundation for all to follow. Understandably he considered *Sinaiticus* as the most reliable of all texts, and this put him in direct conflict with the *Received Text*. Samuel Tregelles followed with a meticulous study of all available material and by 1872 produced a Greek Text which was published after his death in 1879. He was little concerned with the *Received Text* although his sole purpose was that his text would be 'for the service of God by serving his church.'

In 1881 the two New Testament scholars from Cambridge, Brooke Fosse Westcott and Fenton John Anthony Hort, put forward a text based almost entirely upon *Sinaiticus* and *Vaticanus*. They assumed, among much else, that because these two texts were much older than the Byzantine texts behind the *Received Text*, they should have precedence. Their preference was for *Vaticanus*. They also made use of the available versions and the writing of the early church leaders to ascertain what they considered the most authentic text. Westcott and Hort were critical, but not wholly dismissive, of the *Received Text*. This was almost universally adopted for many years and few dared to disagree with it for fear of not being considered scholarly. Even the conservative A T Robertson,[76] and the staunch defender of biblical inerrancy, Benjamin B Warfield, followed the Westcott and Hort approach.

It should be noted that the ten to twenty percent of texts outside the *Majority Text* family do not all agree with each other, and the fact that *Sinaiticus* and others are older than the *Received Text* does not necessarily make them more accurate.

---

76 A T Robertson, *Introduction to the Textual Criticism of the New Testament* (Sunday School Board of the Southern Convention, New York, 1925): 'It is worthwhile to explain precisely what the *Textus Receptus* is so that students may know at the very outset why it cannot now be followed', p. 17. Although he did concede that the *Textus Receptus* was 'substantially correct.'

The position of Westcott and Hort was vigorously attacked by John Burgon, Dean of Chichester, who considered *Sinaiticus*, *Vaticanus* and *Bezae*: 'three of the most scandalously corrupt copies extant',[77] but he was almost alone. Other scholars, like Scrivener and Salmon, pointed out that whilst Westcott and Hort had made a valuable contribution, they were quite wrong to disregard the Byzantine (*Received Text*) and Western texts to the extent they did.

Some have tried to accuse *Sinaiticus* and *Vaticanus* of coming from the pen of scribes seeking to deny the full deity of Christ, but this is wholly unjustified, not least because if it is true, those scribes made a strange blunder at John 1:18. Here *Sinaiticus* and *Vaticanus* both speak of Christ as 'the only begotten God', whereas the *Received Text* has merely 'the only begotten Son'. The difference is between *theos* and *uios* in the Greek; an illustration of how possible it is for a scribe to make a slight, but significant, mistake.

The *Revised Version* of 1881 was the first translation to adopt the Westcott and Hort text for the New Testament translation as it was found in Alexander Souter's *Novum Testamentum Graece*.

THE 'ECLECTIC' TEXT

Many have preferred to avoid the rigid boundaries of accepting only the *Received Text* or that of Westcott and Hort, and they steer a middle course following evangelical scholars both of the past and the present. Godly textual scholarship should not be opposed in its attempt to find the best text resulting from the evaluation of everything that is available. This is called an 'eclectic' text, that is, using all sources. A preference for the *Received Text* would therefore not prevent using the evidence of other valuable texts.

This is not the place to enter the detailed debate concerning the rigorous 'rules' that govern the science of textual criticism. It is by far the most complex of all the biblical sciences. But sufficient to say that there are well established procedures that are used for discussing the

---

77 J W Burgon, *The Revision Revised* (London. 1883), p. 16.

texts of any piece of literature from Homer to Shakespeare. Nor is it a new science. Early in the third century Origen compiled his *Hexapla*, a presentation of the Old Testament Hebrew and Greek texts in six columns, and this was studied by scholars well into the seventh century until it was destroyed by the forces of Islam in the general pillage of the great libraries of the east.

For centuries, the Roman Catholic hierarchy would allow only the Latin *Vulgate* to be used and was convinced that it was the only reliable and accurate text. Strictly this is still the position of Rome, and any translation has to be based upon the Latin *Vulgate*. We should be cautious about giving any one text an infallibility above all others. More texts are available to us today than were available even to Westcott and Hort.

Examples of Textual criticism

MARK 16:9–20

In the pursuit of the best text, possibly no other passage in the New Testament has received such close attention as this one. Many monographs have been published and at least one doctorate has been earned by grappling with it. The evidence, briefly stated, is that these twelve verses are not found in our two oldest Greek codices, *Sinaiticus* and *Vaticanus*, nor in some of the versions (early translations); in addition, some have discovered in these verses seventeen words that either Mark uses nowhere else or are used here in a different sense.

On the other hand, the verses are included in all the other Greek manuscripts, in all the early Latin manuscripts except one, and are quoted as Scripture by many early church leaders who lived even before *Sinaiticus* and *Vaticanus* were copied. It is found in Justin Martyr (c. 165), Tatian (c. 170), Irenaeus (c. 202) and Hippolytus (c. 235). Having said this, Jerome (c. 419) when he was preparing the Latin *Vulgate* stated: 'Almost all the Greek copies [available to him] do not have this concluding portion.'

Whether or not the evidence is in favour of keeping Mark 16:9–20 where it is, at the end of Mark's Gospel, one thing is certain: it is not a matter of indifference whether these verses are part of Scripture; it is essential that we have good reasons either to keep them in or to leave them out. Some translations will add a note to this passage that it is not found in 'The most reliable early manuscripts and other ancient witnesses' (NIV 1984). The claim 'most reliable manuscripts' is a judgement that not all scholars would agree with. The ESV (2001) notes, 'Some of the earliest manuscripts do not include...' which is fair and accurate.

JOHN 7:53 TO 8:11

Unlike the above passage in Mark this section, known as the *pericope adulterae*, is not referred to by most of the early church leaders. It is not found in the texts of *Sinaiticus*, *Alexandrinus* and *Vaticanus* nor in many of the older versions (translations). A few texts even place it after John 21:25 or after Luke 21.

On the other side of the debate, in the fourth century, Eusebius commented that Papias (martyred in AD 135) expounded from it.[78] So it was evidently known in the second century. Augustine claimed that some removed it from their texts for fear that it would give women an excuse for their immoral behaviour.[79] He was therefore familiar with it in the late fourth century.

It is certainly in the *Majority Text* and in the *Vulgate* of Jerome. It is also found in some early versions, including a sixth century Syriac, an Egyptian (Coptic), and an Ethiopic version, and *Codex Bezae*.

We may add that the passage fits well into the context of John's Gospel at this point (though some dispute this) and, more especially, it has all the hallmarks of an eyewitness account as the literary scholar C S Lewis observed.[80] There is no reason for such an account to have been 'invented', and a persuasive argument can be made to support the suggestion that it was deliberately left out of the Eastern texts because of Jesus' mild rebuke to the woman.

---

78 Eusebius, *Ecclesiastical History*, Book 3.39:17. Eusebius claims that he found it in the 'Gospel according to the Hebrews.' This 'Gospel' has not survived.
79 Augustine, *De adulterinis conjugiis*, II: vii.
80 C S Lewis, Essay: *What are we to make of Jesus Christ?* 1950.

Of all passages in the New Testament, this is one of the most contentious.[81]

1 TIMOTHY 3:16

In contrast to a discussion of a lengthy passage, we can turn to one where a single word is in dispute.

In the *New International Version* (1984), part of 1 Timothy 3:16 reads: 'Beyond all question, the mystery of godliness is great: He appeared in a body...' A footnote adds, 'Some manuscripts read God' in place of 'he'. What the translators do not tell us is that three hundred Greek manuscripts read 'God', six read 'who', two read 'he', and one reads 'which'! Many translations have 'he' because the translators believe that *Codex Sinaiticus* and the other manuscripts and versions where this word is found have the best reading at this point. The *English Standard Version* (2001) follows this also.

However, the fact that some later corrections to *Sinaiticus* have the word 'God', as do most later Greek manuscripts and a number of versions, means that there is a strong case to be made for the word 'God'. Why the difference? Since the words 'who', 'he' and 'which' are quite similar in the Greek (even more so when, as is the case here, abbreviations are used), a scribe might well have confused them. 'God' is a very distinct word and likely, therefore, to be the original. But some think the scribe may have allowed his eye to wander to the verse he had just written (v. 15), where the word 'God' appears twice, and he mistakenly copied it in at verse 16 also. Alternatively a helpful scribe might even have changed 'he' to 'God' in order to make it clear who 'he' is!

A judgement has to be made on which evidence we believe is best, but most readers do not have the skill for this and have to rely on the translators. Fortunately, not many passages are up for discussion in this way, as we have already noted; and even this one in 1 Timothy 3:16

---

81 For a brief defence of its authenticity see William Hendriksen (1954), *Gospel of John* (Banner of Truth, Edinburgh, 1976), Ch. 8. For a more detailed discussion of the subject against its inclusion, with all the texts listed, see Philip W Comfort, *New Testament Text and Translation Commentary* (Tyndale House Publishers Inc., Illinois, 2008), pp. 285–288.

does not affect our theology. If the word is 'God' then clearly we have evidence that Christ who 'appeared in a body' was God. If the word is 'he' then it can only refer to the 'living God' who is referred to in the previous verse and who we are now told 'appeared in a body'. If there was a helpful scribe trying to make it clear that 'he' refers to God, he need not have bothered since there is no other way to understand the passage.

ACTS 6:8

The *Majority Text* here reads 'Stephen, a man full of God's faith (*pisteos*) and power' whereas the Eastern family of texts, including *Sinaiticus*, *Alexandrinus*, *Vaticanus* and *Bezae* all read 'grace (*charitos*) and power'. The two words are not easy to confuse, so why the difference? It is possible that a scribe was influenced by the reference in verse 5 to Stephen 'full of *faith*' and inadvertently wrote that instead of 'grace'.

REVELATION 1:5,6

In the sentence: 'To him who *loves* us and has *freed* us from our sins by his blood, and has made us to be a *kingdom* and priests to serve his God and Father', there are three small textual variations highlighted here by the words in italics. The first concerns the word *loves*. Some Greek texts have the past tense 'loved', whilst others have the present tense 'loves'. There is, of course, no difference in substantial meaning, for if he loved us then he still loves, and if he loves, it is only because he first loved us. The difference is between the *Received Text*—*agapomen* (loved) and the text of *Sinaiticus*—*agaponti* (loves).

The second variation is between the *Received Text*—*lousanti* (washed) and *Sinaiticus*—*lusanti* (freed), a single letter changes the meaning of the word. But both truths are well established elsewhere in Scripture.

The third is the difference between *basileis* (kings) and *basileian* (kingdom), again a small change in two letters, but no clash of meaning. It may be thought that 'kings' is better since it precedes the noun 'priests'; the opposite view would be that 'kingdom' is not what we would expect and therefore it is less likely that a copyist would make a mistake.

1 JOHN 1:4

Here we have the difference between 'our joy' and 'your joy'. The difference in the Greek is as close as it is in the English—just one letter. A scribe copying from dictation might hear it incorrectly or, in the afternoon weariness of a hard day scribing, his hand might inadvertently pen the wrong word. The difference is minimal. This is the level of the great majority of textual issues in the New Testament. The availability of so many texts generally enables the scholar to determine what the true text ought to be.

JOHN 3:16

The variation in some translations: 'his only Son' or 'his only begotten Son' is not a textual matter at all. All Greek texts read the same here. It is a question of whether the Greek word *monogenes* means simply 'one and only' or 'only begotten'. The consensus of scholars limits its use to 'one and only'.[82] Nothing is affected by the differences since the New Testament is clear that the Father has only one Son and that he was begotten through the virgin Mary.

CONCLUSION

These short exercises are what is meant by 'textual criticism'. Often the context will help us decide the best text to follow. We may be assured that although textual criticism, and the assessment of the material available, is a complex and highly academic task, all but a tiny fraction of the New Testament is unquestioned on any ground, and no doctrine or historical fact hangs upon a disputed passage. It is not generally appreciated that all the main doctrinal passages of the New Testament are entirely free from any textual problem. It may appear alarming to be told that a twentieth century edition of the Greek text designed for translators contains 1,440 variant readings 'chosen especially in view of their exegetical significance',[83] but it was Westcott himself who unhesitatingly declared

---

82 See for example Arndt and Gingrich (trans. Walter Bauer), *A Greek-English Lexicon of the New Testament* (1979); and Moulton and Milligan, *Vocabulary of the Greek New Testament* (1930).
83 Metzger, *The Text of the New Testament* (OUP, Oxford 1992), third ed. p. 146.

that all the differences did not amount to more than a 'thousandth part' of the whole New Testament. A significant proportion of the variants are limited to a single word. There are almost 8,000 verses in the Greek New Testament made up of over 138,000 words.

The New Testament is unique for the amount of ancient material available, and no one can doubt that in all but a few areas we can be certain of the words of the original text. However, we must not underestimate the significance of any passage in which equally valuable manuscripts differ. The doctrine of verbal inspiration can never allow us to call any difference 'insignificant', even if it is only a dispute over 'your' or 'our', 'he' or 'who'. But what is equally true is that we may safely turn to our Greek New Testament and be sure that it reflects accurately in verbal form the mind of God. Where there are difficulties we must with honesty admit our limited knowledge at that point. The problems of textual criticism need never cause us to turn aside from a belief in verbal and plenary inspiration.

More recently, Bruce Metzger, a cautious scholar of the New Testament text, after outlining some of the inevitable errors that do creep in after centuries of copying, added this important caveat: 'Lest the foregoing examples of alterations should give the impression that scribes were altogether wilful and capricious in transmitting ancient copies of the New Testament, it ought to be noted that other evidence points to the careful and painstaking work on the part of many faithful copyists. There are, for example, instances of difficult readings which have been transmitted with scrupulous fidelity.'[84] He then provides a few examples where an obvious grammatical blunder has been faithfully transcribed by a copyist who would not dare to change the text in front of him and concludes: 'These examples of dogged fidelity on the part of scribes could be multiplied.'

Much earlier, Sir Frederick Kenyon, Director of the British Museum for twenty-one years, expressed his own confidence in the Bible text like this: 'The Christian can take the whole Bible in his hand and say

---

84 Bruce Metzger, above, p. 206.

without fear or hesitation that he holds in it the true word of God, handed down without essential loss from generation to generation throughout the centuries.'[85]

All the evidence that has come to light since Sir Frederick Kenyon wrote that reinforces the claim.

---

[85] F Kenyon, *Our Bible and the Ancient Manuscripts* (London 1895), p. 55.

5. Which translation?

'What is the best translation?' is one of the most common questions. The answer is often a matter of prejudice or preference—but there are some basic rules to govern our choice.

In this chapter we will take up the story of the Bible in English where we left it at the end of chapter one, and then discuss how we can choose between the many translations and paraphrases available. This chapter will not be comprehensive, because the total number of translations of the complete Bible into English since John Wycliffe at the end of the fourteenth century reaches, by some calculations, over three hundred and fifty!

Beyond the *King James Version*

From the seventeenth century, the Bible shaped not only the religious and social life of the nation but every aspect of life, from science to politics. For half a century from the Restoration of the Monarchy in 1660 the *King James Version* held sway with many imprints but with few revisions. The Bible was the foundation of the emerging missionary societies of the early nineteenth century, and in its first eleven years of activity from 1804, the British and Foreign Bible Society could report that it had distributed almost half a million copies of the complete Bible and as many New Testaments—all in the *King James Version*.

The eighteenth century saw several revisions of the *King James Authorized Version* for example: Whitby in 1703, Wells in 1718–24, Whiston in 1745 and Blayney in 1769. In 1768 even John Wesley produced a revision with notes for 'plain, unlettered men who understand only their Mother Tongue'. Wesley carefully studied the Greek and made about twelve thousand alterations, all of which he considered necessary.

In 1729 Daniel Mace, a Presbyterian minister and able scholar, offered his own New Translation with the Greek alongside it. It was a brave attempt to update the already dated language of parts of the *King James Version*, but was little acknowledged and soon passed into silent history. During this century, additional Greek texts were coming to light with occasional variant readings from the fourth revision of the *Received Text* (*Textus Receptus*) by Robert Estienne in 1551, that lay behind the *King James Version*. Daniel Mace had used an eclectic Greek text (all that was available to him) for his translation and this was one reason why his work was ignored.

The first major challenge to the *Received Text* came in 1777 with the publication of a Greek text of the New Testament compiled by Johann Jakob Griesbach in Germany. In addition to references from the early church Fathers where they quoted from New Testament books, and old versions (translations into Armenian, Gothic, Syriac), Griesbach used the latest Greek texts that had been discovered. He was followed by others, but his remained the standard text for a century until Westcott and Hort brought out an even more eclectic text in 1881 which formed the basis of the *Revised Version* of the Bible. See the previous chapter for details of the development of the Greek text.

By the nineteenth century full use was being made of the Greek manuscripts that were not available to the 1611 translators. *Codex Alexandrinus* for example (see Book 4 chapter 3 in this series), arrived in England just sixteen years too late for King James' translation teams, and it is debatable how much use they would have made of it had they had access. Many more followed. Translations and paraphrases continued including: Sharpe in 1840 and 1865, Young in 1862, Conybeare and Howson in 1864, Dean Alford in 1869, J N Darby in 1871 and 1890, Rotherham 1872 and 1897–1902, and Newberry in 1890.

Although the *King James Version* had served the nation well for many centuries, it was not merely the new texts that prompted a revision. The change of language and a better understanding of some Hebrew and Greek words meant that a more accurate translation was possible. One example can highlight this: John Wycliffe in 1388, William Tyndale in 1526 , the *Geneva Bible* in 1560 and the *King James Version* in 1611 all translated the Greek word *theopneustos* in 2 Timothy 3:16 by the word 'inspired'; this was the only occasion the word appeared in the Greek New Testament. However, by the early twentieth century the word *theopneustos* was far better understood. B B Warfield, Professor of Theology at Princeton Seminary in New Jersey from 1887–1921, had made a meticulously academic study of the word in all its uses outside the Bible. His conclusion was that it was a passive word meaning 'breathed out' and not an active word 'breathing into'.[86] For this reason, 'God-breathed', referring to the ultimate origin of Scripture, was a far better translation than 'inspired' which referred to the method of transmitting Scripture to men. This is now accepted by almost all modern translations. See in this series Book 2 chapter 2 'The meaning of "inspiration"'.

Making a choice

TRANSLATION OR PARAPHRASE?

Throughout the following survey, a distinction is made between translations, revisions and paraphrases. A *translation* goes back to the original Hebrew and Greek and attempts to give the meaning of the words in the nearest equivalent English. A revision is based upon an existing translation and, though the revisers will consult the original Hebrew and Greek, their main aim will be to update the language of the translation and correct any errors. A revision may still be a translation. A *paraphrase* attempts to give the meaning rather than the words of the original writer; it therefore loosely translates thoughts rather than words. A paraphrase will change words, phrases and idioms to make the text easy to understand. A paraphrase can never be described as an accurate translation and, however readable it may be, it should not be used as a serious study Bible either privately or publicly. Even among translations, there is a difference between 'formal equivalence and 'dynamic equivalence'. The first being a translation as close as possible to the words used in the original, whereas the second looks for the best

---

86 B B Warfield, *The Inspiration and Authority of the Bible* (The Presbyterian and Reformed Publishing Company, Philadelphia 1948), pp. 245–296.

equivalent in the receiving ('receptor') language. In reality, no translation stays unerringly with one position or the other.

TRANSLATING FROM THE BEST TEXT

The most important starting point is whether the version is based on the best possible original texts. This is not so much an issue with the Old Testament, since all will rely upon the Hebrew *Masoretic Text* with only occasional use of the *Septuagint*, the *Dead Sea Scrolls* and other ancient versions. See in this series Book 3 chapter 2 and here chapter 2. For the New Testament, readers must make their preference based on the various approaches that were outlined in the previous chapter. The underlying text used in most modern translations (the *New King James Version* being an exception) will be an 'eclectic' text—using all the available material. However, it is wise to bear in mind that whether the text used by the translators is the *Received Text* (*Majority Text*), the Westcott and Hort text, or an eclectic text, the differences are, with a few exceptions, minimal. Differences between one translation and another are overwhelmingly a different rendering of the same Greek word.

At times, words in the original Hebrew or Greek can be left untranslated, or words need to be added, to make sense in the receiving language. All translations, including the *King James Version*, do this frequently.

TRANSLATING TO BE READ

Although the underlying text is important, a translation to be used publicly should read well. From Wycliffe to the *Geneva Bible* via Tyndale, the attempt was always to make God's word read so plainly that, as Tyndale declared in 1521 (and Erasmus before him in 1516), even the boy who drives the plough would understand it. The Jew would go to the temple and later the synagogue to hear the Torah being read. He did not have the Hebrew Scriptures (our Old Testament) on a scroll at home. It was the same with the early Christians; the great expense of copying the letters of Paul, for example, prohibited any but the most wealthy from owning their own copies. Justin Martyr, around AD 150, informs us that on Sunday 'all who live in cities or in the country gather together to one place, and the memoirs of the apostles or the writings of the prophets are read, as long as time permits; then, when the reader has ceased, the president verbally instructs, and exhorts to the imitation of these good things.'[87]

The Bible was written in the common language of the people of its day, whether Hebrew or Greek. The New Testament is written not in classical Attic Greek, but in Koine Greek—the language of the people. This should indicate that we need a translation that is in the language of today, and since language is rarely static—especially the English language which is both rich and changing—new translations, or at least revisions, will be required from time to time. Few people speak in seventeenth century language today unless they are on stage. However, this does not mean that we should convert chariots into tanks and bows into AK-47s, because it is important to retain the cultural setting of Bible times. Generally, we must translate what Isaiah or Paul wrote *then*, not how they would have written it today. Although occasionally there have to be exceptions to this. To translate Judges 5:30 'a womb or two for each man' (*English Standard Version*, 2001) may be precise but it is not very helpful for a congregation, when 'a girl or two' (*New International Version*, 1983) would be more sensible.

No translation can translate exactly word for word without it becoming meaningless and unreadable. Dr Fisher provides an example of a literal translation of the Hebrew of Genesis 33:14: 'As for me, let me lead my gentleness to the foot of the business which is to my face and to the foot of the children that I shall come to my lord to Seir.'[88] Similarly, Genesis 34:26 literally speaks of the 'mouth of the sword', but the 'edge of the sword' is more sensible.

A good translation will stay as close as possible to the words of the original and will avoid interpreting or explaining a difficult passage. The translator translates; the expositor (preacher or teacher) explains. However, the translator must be aware when a word in the original has a different meaning depending upon the context in which it is used. The

---

87 Justin Martyr, *First Apology* addressed to the emperor Titus, ch. 67.
88 Dr J C Fisher in *The New Testament Student and Bible Translation*, Ed. J H Skilton (Presbyterian and Reformed Publishing Co., Phillipsburg 1978), p. 31.

translator must also ensure that the Scriptures read easily in the best prose that an accurate translation will allow. The repetition of small words, like 'and' for example, that may be in the text but are not necessary to translate, becomes tedious when read publicly.

TRANSLATING THE CULTURE

In the attempt to persuade a generation of non-readers to take up a Bible, there is a danger of being more concerned with those who read it than those who wrote it. It is true that the Bible, written long ago in cultures very different from our own, requires some understanding of its context. That is the roll of the preacher/teacher. But the claim that the Bible has a different 'voltage' from today and therefore requires a 'transformer', has led some to conclude that communicating the message is more important than accuracy of translation. This is a false distinction. Translators must never forget that primarily they are responsible for the *text* of Scripture, not its *meaning*. To translate the 'Sabbath day's journey' (Acts 1:12) by 'about a kilometre' (*Good News Bible* and *New Living Translation*, though the latter has a footnote), or 'the half mile' (*Living Bible*), is to reduce the Bible to a flat, cultureless handbook. In this case, it also obscures an important point of culture. The 'Sabbath day's journey' was the limit of travel strictly allowed by the Pharisees on the Sabbath day. The *New International Version* (NIV), the *New King James Version* (NKJV), the *English Standard Version* (ESV) and others, are wise to retain the phrase and provide a footnote that informs the reader of the modern equivalent.

It is even more unhelpful to replace shekels and denarii with modern equivalents, since money values change rapidly. Besides, the denarius (Matthew 22:19) was important as the daily wage of a labourer or a Roman legionary. Even weights and measures are best left in since, across the English-speaking world, these are expressed differently. Footnotes (or a conversion table) to give equivalents are the better alternative.

Modern English does not use the second person singular. The argument in favour of 'thee' and 'thou' as a reverent or respectful way of addressing Deity is no more than a well-meaning personal preference. There is no such distinction in the Hebrew or Greek of the Scriptures. Even Satan is addressed by the second person singular.

TRANSLATING THEOLOGY

There are many significant words in the Christian vocabulary that must be retained. Words like election, atonement, justification, sanctification and grace can lose their theological distinction if they are not retained.

An important example of this is the word 'propitiation'. It is a vital word in Christian theology for the meaning of the cross, especially as the writers give a whole new meaning from that of the first century pagan understanding. Propitiation referred to human efforts to placate the disinterest or anger of the gods. In the New Testament, it is God's way of satisfying his own just anger against our rebellion. The word appears (as a noun or verb) in only five verses of the New Testament (Romans 3:25; Hebrews 2:17; 9:5; 1 John 2:2; 4:10) and some translators have found it hard to deal with because there is no adequate English synonym, and yet they realise it is not commonly used today. The *Revised Standard Version* uses the word 'expiation' and the *New International Version* 'a sacrifice of atonement' neither of which get to the heart of the original Greek noun *hilastèrion*. The *Good News Bible* has a clumsy and wholly inadequate paraphrase for the single word: 'God offered him so that by his death he should become the means by which people's sins are forgiven.' The *Living Bible* and *New Living Translation* get to the heart of its meaning but with an equally long sentence: 'to take the punishment for our sins and to end all God's anger against us.' Wisely, the *King James Version*, *New King James Version*, *Revised Version*, *New American Standard Bible* and the *English Standard Version* all retain 'propitiation' since it is a theological word that should not be lost.

TRANSLATING GENDER

The English translator in the twenty-first century is confronted with the demand for 'gender-neutral' language. This is often taken to foolish extremes in our contemporary culture, but Bible translators must be wise and sensitive. Wisdom is to know when the masculine is deliberate or simply a general reference to men and women. In English 'mankind' is always generic and to change it to 'human kind' (which still retains the word 'man') is unnecessary. However, the centuries-old use of 'men' meaning 'people' and 'he' referring to anyone of either sex is no longer acceptable. There is generally a clear distinction in the Greek between *aner*, meaning a man, and *anthropos*, meaning people generally. For this reason, it is perfectly proper for Acts 17:30 to render the word *anthropos* by 'he commands all people everywhere to repent'.

A more difficult decision is how to translate *adelphos* and *adelphoi* (brother and brothers). This masculine noun is frequently used, especially in the letters of Paul, and it can sometimes be generic for brothers and sisters. There is evidence for this outside the Bible also. Some would suggest that in Luke 21:16 clearly both brothers and sisters are implied: 'You will be betrayed even by parents, brothers, relatives and friends…'.

However, the decision to translate *adelphoi* with 'brothers and sisters' assumes we are certain when Paul is not addressing only the men; this is debatable. In 1 Corinthians *adelphoi* occurs twenty-seven times and one translation uses 'brother and sisters' on twenty-one occasions. A case could be made that in most instances Paul is specifically addressing the leaders of the church, who would be men. Strict adherence to this gender sensitive translation occasionally presents oddities. For example, in 1 Corinthians 7:29, to translate 'brothers' by 'brothers and sisters' is strange when clearly the men are being addressed since the same verse refers to 'those who have wives'. Some translators make the decision at 1 Corinthians 6:6 that Paul meant only 'one *brother* takes another to court' (NIV 2011) rather than 'one brother or sister', whereas the 'brothers' in 1 Corinthians 16:20 is translated 'brothers and sisters'. The *New Living Translation* replaces 'brother' in 1 Corinthians 6:6 with 'Christian', which is oddly misleading since Paul never used the word 'Christian' in his letters.

It should be noted that there are occasions when the feminine (*adelphē*) is coupled with the masculine to make it clear that both are meant—for example in Mark 3:35 and James 2:15—therefore the New Testament writers used both men and women (*adelphoi adelphē*) when they wanted to.

Gender sensitive translations mean that some phrases embedded in Christian language lose their impact. 'I will make you fishers of men' (Matthew 4:19) becomes 'I will send you out to fish for people.' The play on words in the previous reference to the disciples being 'fishermen' is therefore lost.

Few will be ready to tamper with the title of Christ as the 'Son of Man' which occurs in Matthew's Gospel alone some fifteen times. This was plainly a Messianic title and Hebrews 2:6 picks it up from Psalm 8:4. However, see under the *New International Version* 2011 below. God is always addressed by masculine pronouns and there are some from the feminist lobby who would like this changed also.

A translation that is 'gender sensitive' treads a very delicate path to be relevant, consistent and accurate. Some words can easily be accommodated, but to go too far will move into the path of exposition rather than translation. It may be questioned whether it is the task of the translator to decide in all cases whether a masculine noun or pronoun is specific or generic.

PRINCIPLES FOR GENDER TRANSLATION

Because the subject of gender language has become so contentious in recent decades, it will be helpful to reproduce some guidelines for translating gender-related language in the Bible. These were affirmed in 1997 by a group representing the main evangelical denominations in the USA and such organizations as Focus on the Family, the Council for Biblical Manhood and Womanhood, and many leading evangelical theologians. These guidelines are not intended to be exhaustive. Examples of each category were given.

A. Gender-related renderings of Biblical language which we affirm:

1. The generic use of 'he, him, his, himself' should be employed to translate generic 3rd person masculine singular pronouns in Hebrew, Aramaic and Greek. However, substantival participles such as *ho pisteuon* can often be rendered in inclusive ways, such as 'the one who believes' rather than 'he who believes.'

2. Person and number should be retained in translation so that singulars are not changed to plurals and third person statements are not changed to second or first person statements, with only rare exceptions required in unusual cases.

3. 'Man' should ordinarily be used to designate the human race, for example in Genesis 1:26-27; 5:2; Ezekiel 29:11; and John 2:25.

4. Hebrew *'ish* should ordinarily be translated 'man' and 'men,' and Greek *aner* should almost always be so translated.

5. In many cases, *anthropoi* refers to people in general, and can be translated 'people' rather than 'men.' The singular *anthropos* should ordinarily be translated 'man' when it refers to a male human being.

6. Indefinite pronouns such as *tis* can be translated 'anyone' rather than 'any man.'

7. In many cases, pronouns such as *oudeis* can be translated 'no one' rather than 'no man.'

8. When *pas* is used as a substantive it can be translated with terms such as 'all people' or 'everyone.'

9. The phrase 'son of man' should ordinarily be preserved to retain intracanonical connections.

10. Masculine references to God should be retained.

B. Gender-related renderings which we will generally avoid, though there may be unusual exceptions in certain contexts:

1. 'Brother' (*adelphos*) should not be changed to 'brother or sister'; however, the plural *adelphoi* can be translated 'brothers and sisters' where the context makes clear that the author is referring to both men and women.

2. 'Son' (*huios*, *ben*) should not be changed to 'child,' or 'sons' (*huioi*) to 'children' or 'sons and daughters.' (However, Hebrew *banim* often means 'children'.)

3. 'Father' (*pater*, *'ab*) should not be changed to 'parent,' or 'fathers' to 'parents' or 'ancestors'.

Which translation?

There are many more translations and paraphrases than are dealt with here, and doubtless more will come. However, these are (or were) some of the most popular and well known. In fairness, it should be stressed that any review of translations will reflect the position and preferences of the reviewer—and what follows is no exception! We should also recognise that no translation or revision will be wholly consistent with its stated intention. No translation is perfect and it is wise to admit this. Since this is the case, it is very easy to single out particular verses or phrases that are poorly translated; this can be done for every translation without exception. However, it is more helpful to refer to the overall translation principles.

THE *REVISED VERSION* (RV)—A REVISION

In 1870, the Upper House of Convocation of the Province of Canterbury agreed to a revision of the *King James Version*, and a committee prepared the ground by listing a number of principles, including the instruction that as few alterations as possible should be introduced into the text of the *King James Version*. In addition, an eclectic text would be used and where this differed from the *King James Version* the alteration would be indicated in the margin. Scholars in the United States of America began a parallel work and it was hoped one version would result. In the event the American Standard Version, free from some of the restrictions placed upon the *Revised Version*, was published separately in 1901.

The *Revised Version* New Testament was ready in 1881 and the Old Testament by 1885. Sales were enormous, and so was opposition, especially by the brilliant Oxford scholar Dean John Burgon. The *Revised Version* was largely the product of men unsympathetic to a conservative approach to the Bible and this was evident in some of the footnotes casting doubt upon portions of Scripture. Many mourned the loss of the dignified *King James Version* language and style: for example, 'the interrogation of a good conscience' is hardly a helpful translation of 1 Peter 3:21. The *Revised Version* achieved little advance upon the

King James Version in the New Testament, and hence it did not remain a popular challenge for long because it was soon overshadowed by the *American Revised Standard Version*.

THE *AMERICAN REVISED STANDARD VERSION* (RSV)—A REVISION

This is a revision of the 1901 *American Standard Version* and the work began in 1937 using 'the best results of modern scholarship.' However, because the translators used an eclectic Greek text (though mainly Westcott and Hort), they were at times too ready to relegate passages like Mark 16:9–20 and John 8:1–11 to a footnote.

The New Testament was published in 1946 and the whole Bible in 1952. It was a great improvement upon the *Revised Version* in terms of style and readable English. The language was modernized: 'saith' becomes 'says', 'sendeth' becomes 'sends' and so on. 'Thou' becomes 'you', except when God is addressed; although the revisers would have saved themselves some criticism if they had not made this exception, since their decision to make the disciples refer to Christ as 'you' during his earthly ministry is a matter of the translators' opinion. In fact, the original Greek knows of no such 'reverent' language when addressing Deity. Quotation marks were introduced for direct speech, and the printing of prophetic statements as poetry was included. For these reasons the *Revised Standard Version* ('American' soon dropped off) achieved a more consistent usage in public than the *Revised Version*.

One of the most serious criticisms levelled against the RSV was that it attempted to downgrade the full deity of Christ, thus reflecting the liberal theology of many of its translators. In places this criticism is valid—there is no justification for 'your divine throne' in Psalm 45:6 (though the expression is correctly translated in Hebrews 1:8 'Thy throne, O God'). More instances are cited but not always with justification. On the other hand, the translation of Titus 2:13, 'awaiting our blessed hope, the appearing of the glory of our great God and Saviour Jesus Christ', and 2 Peter 1:1, 'the righteousness of our God and Saviour Jesus Christ', unquestionably affirm the true deity of Christ, precisely where the *King James Version* obscures it.

The RSV had much to commend it at the time. There were some poor translations, but it had the advantage of being generally more careful than the AV in translating particular words. For example, the AV obscures the difference between 'creatures' in Revelation 4 and 'beast' in Revelation 13—two entirely different Greek words are used, which the RSV makes clear. Similarly, the *King James Version* frequently translates the word *daimonion* as 'devil'. But the words 'demon' and 'devil' are not the same; the RSV gives the correct word (demons) in Matthew 8:31; 1 Timothy 4:1 and James 2:19, for example.

With the greater appreciation of the Hebrew language since 1611, the RSV was better able to render some of the previously unknown phrases and words. Thus, the totally meaningless 'The flood breaketh out from the inhabitant; even the waters forgotten of the foot: they are dried up, they are gone way from men' of Job 28:4 (*King James Version*) becomes 'They open shafts in a valley away from where men live; they are forgotten by travellers, they hang afar from men, they swing to and fro.' We now know that Job is talking about mining deep beneath the earth.

For some years the RSV was very popular among evangelical Christians—even though it was justifiably criticised for, among other things, substituting the word 'expiation' in place of 'propitiation'. It at least provided a more 'modern' translation.

NEW AMERICAN STANDARD BIBLE—A TRANSLATION

'On July 31st 1970 the *New American Standard Bible* was completed after 9 years and 7 months of intensive work by 58 consecrated and dedicated scholars'—so reads the cover blurb of this translation published by the Lockman Foundation of California. The translators all believed 'the words of Scripture as originally penned in the Hebrew and Greek were inspired by God.' The Greek text is based largely on the Nestle Greek New Testament, which is an eclectic text, and this made it more acceptable among many evangelicals than those based solely upon Westcott and Hort.

Punctuation and paragraphs were changed to clarify the meaning of the passage. Personal pronouns commence with a capital when referring to the Deity, and the second singular ('thou', 'thy' and 'thee') are retained when the Deity is addressed. On this latter point the NASB follows the *Revised Standard Version* in using 'you' to refer to Christ prior to his ascension; this is an unwise approach for it necessitates a decision when and where the speaker knew he was addressing Christ as God. The rendering of Luke 1:3 as 'consecutive order' is a hostage to fortune since by 'an orderly account' Luke meant simply a meaningful order; 'consecutive order' may present problems in view of the different order of events in the Gospels.

Generally, the NASB is a good translation, and words added to bring out the sense are faithfully placed in italics. There is a dignity in style and language that commends this version to public use, provided that the use of the second singular is no barrier. Readers who are looking for a formal translation for serious study, ('propitiation' is retained in Romans 3:25 for example), and are willing to sacrifice a little readability to gain it, will find this an excellent translation. It has, however, been overtaken by more recent translations.

J B PHILLIPS—A PARAPHRASE

J B Phillips completed his paraphrase by 1957 and for a time it was very popular, even amongst evangelical Christians, who were often unaware that Phillips denied Bible inerrancy and reserved the right to 'expand or explain' the text.[89] He did this with sometimes disastrous results. In Matthew 7:12, 'This is the law and the prophets', becomes 'This is the essence of all true religion.' In Luke 6:37, 'Forgive and you shall be forgiven,' becomes 'Make allowances for others and people will make allowances for you.' Similarly, 'When he shall appear we shall be like him' (1 John 3:2) becomes: 'If reality were to break through, we should reflect his likeness...' In 1 Corinthians 14:22 the whole verse is revised into what Phillips thought Paul meant to say! Perhaps it is fortunate that Philips has long been neglected, though at the time it was popular among undiscerning evangelicals.

---

89 See Book 5 chapter 1 in this series for Phillips' view of inerrancy.

THE *NEW WORLD TRANSLATION*

The *New World Translation* is the Bible of the Watchtower Bible and Tract Society (Jehovah's Witnesses) and is the only translation produced by a cult. It was completed in 1960 and revised in 1961, but the names, and therefore the qualifications, of the translators were never officially revealed. Subtle changes are made to the text to agree with Watchtower doctrine, and this is seen most clearly in the attempts to avoid the deity of Christ. However, it is only in the large library edition that these changes are admitted. We are not surprised that John 1:1 is rendered, 'The Word was a god', by a cult that does not believe in the deity of Christ, but there is much more obvious manipulation of the text. In Colossians 2:9–10 the word *theotetos* is translated 'In him all the fullness of the divine quality dwells', yet in Romans 1:20 a related word is accurately translated 'Godship'. *The Watchtower* admits: 'The way these words have been rendered in the *New World Translation* has given rise to the charge that the New World Bible Translation Committee let their religious beliefs influence them. That charge is true, but they did not do so wrongly or unduly. The meaning that is to be given to these two Greek words depends upon what the entire Bible has to say about Jehovah God and Jesus Christ.'[90]

Titus 2:13 is translated: '…we wait for the happy hope and glorious manifestation of the great God and of our Saviour Christ Jesus.' There is no manuscript evidence for the genitive, 'of' before 'our Saviour', and without it the deity of Christ is plainly stated. The library edition provides a lengthy statement to justify the inclusion of the genitive, offering only Moffatt and obscure German, French and Spanish translations (all by individuals) as evidence, but admitting that it is inserted to avoid attributing deity to Christ.[91] Similarly, 2 Peter 1:1 is rendered: '… of our God and *the* Saviour Jesus Christ'. The library edition footnote admits there is no evidence for the definite article but it is inserted 'to agree with the distinction between God and Jesus in the next verse'.[92] The NWT does

---

90 *The Watchtower*, August 1962, p. 480.
91 The *New World Translation*, library edition (Watchtower Bible and Tract Society, New York 1961), Appendix p. 3592.
92 As above, p. 3480.

not indicate by brackets or italics (as here) that the words 'of' and 'the' have been added.

Another example of interpretation rather than translation is found in the rendering of the word 'worship'. The Greek word (*proskuneo*) appears fifty-nine times in the New Testament and with two exceptions (Matthew 18:26; Acts 10:25) is used only with reference to God, Christ or the false worship of idols and demons. The *New World Translation* consistently uses 'obeisance' when it refers to Christ and 'worship' when it refers to God the Father or demons or idols.

The *New World Translation* library edition provides 'a concordance of all the places in this translation where the name Jehovah occurs in the Christian Greek Scriptures'.[93] This is odd to say the least, since there is no word in the Greek New Testament that is the equivalent of Jehovah— which in itself is not an Old Testament Hebrew word. The Greek word for 'Lord' is *kurios*. The *New World Translation* chooses to translate *kurios* by 'Jehovah' when it refers to God the Father and by 'Lord' when it refers to Christ. That is interpretation and not translation.

This alone is sufficient evidence that the Watchtower Movement cannot honestly deny that their translation has deliberately manipulated the text of Scripture to fit their theology.

THE *AMPLIFIED BIBLE*—A TRANSLATION/PARAPHRASE

Completed in 1962, the *Amplified Bible* endeavoured to bring out the various shades of meaning in the Hebrew and Greek words. The New Testament text was that of Westcott and Hort. A typical example of this amplification is found in John 1:12: 'But to as many as did receive and welcome him, he gave the authority (power, privilege, right) to become the children of God, that is, to those who believe in—adhere to, trust in and rely on—his name.' Clearly this version could never be used for public reading. But it has been useful in private study for those who do not have access to the Hebrew or Greek.

---

93 As above, Appendix p. 1450.

By the use of parenthesis, dashes and brackets, the committee tried to distinguish between additional meanings included in the Greek and Hebrew, and comments intended to clarify the meaning. This often makes for clumsy and even ungrammatical reading. For example, Romans 8:29 reads, 'For those whom he foreknew—of whom he was aware and loved beforehand—he also destined from the beginning (foreordaining them) to be moulded into the image of his son [and share inwardly his likeness], that he might become the first born among many brethren.' But perhaps this does not matter for the intended purpose of the *Amplified Bible*.

THE GOOD NEWS BIBLE—A PARAPHRASE

The *Good News Bible* was published by the American Bible Society in 1976 and was subtitled *Today's English Version* (GNB/TEV). Although it claims to be a translation, it is much closer to a paraphrase. The various editions are adorned with simple line drawings and enjoyed greater publicity than any translation before it. TEV sold by the millions of copies. It was the work basically of one man, Dr Robert Bratcher, who denied both inerrancy and infallibility and went so far as to call the evangelical position 'heresy. From the beginning, significant mistranslations marred it as a serious study Bible. Frequently, and significantly, the reference to the 'blood' of Christ was translated by the word 'death'. In Acts 20:28, for example: 'which he made his own through the death of his Son' should literally be 'which he bought with his own blood'; this is typical of many such instances.

It is equally serious that in Romans 4:3,5,6,9,11,22 the phrase 'God accepted him as righteous,' is repeatedly used. This misses the whole point of imputed righteousness. The Greek word used here is *logizomai* and nowhere can it mean 'to accept'; on the contrary the word means 'to reckon' or 'pass to someone's account', 'to impute'. It is one of Paul's favourite words and he uses it twenty-seven times. Similarly, 'the means by which our sins are forgiven' is a sadly weak translation of *hilasmos* in Romans 3:25 and elsewhere, which is best translated by 'propitiation', and refers to the satisfaction of God's righteous anger against sin. It is wise never to use this poor paraphrase for either public or private study worship.

THE *NEW ENGLISH BIBLE*—A TRANSLATION

The *New English Bible* (NEB), completed in 1970, had as its aim to present the Bible in an English 'which is as clear and natural for the modern reader as the subject matter will allow'. Whether or not it succeeded can be judged by a glance through Paul's two letters to Timothy, where the following words are met: interminable, patricides, matricides, felicity, specious, inculcate, precepts, atrophied, fidelity, craven, adjure, refractory, implacable, insinuate, charlatans, refuting and retribution. In addition, crude colloquialisms abound: 'I sponged on no one' (2 Corinthians 11:9); 'they left me in the lurch' (2 Timothy 4:16); 'they got wind of it' (Acts 14:6); 'it touched them on the raw' (Acts 7:54); 'smashing them to bits' (Revelation 2:27); and in the Old Testament, 'David got wind of it' (1 Samuel 23:25); 'itches for your gift' (Isaiah 1:23); 'you mighty toppers' (Isaiah 5:22). T S Eliot, the essayist, playwright, poet and literary critic, once described the *New English Bible* as 'vulgar, trivial and pedantic'.

There are many examples that represent the doctrinal weakness of the translators. 'Every inspired Scripture has its use for...' (2 Timothy 3:16), implies that not all Scripture is inspired; in 1 John 2:2 'propitiation' becomes a weak 'remedy for the defilement of our sins'; and in Isaiah 9:6 the magnificent Hebrew expression, 'Mighty God' (*El Gibbor*) becomes merely 'Godlike'.

In 1989 the *Revised English Bible* was published as 'a fundamental revision of the *New English Bible*'. It was planned to be acceptable 'to all Christians' and certainly it had the support of the mainline denominations including the Baptist Union of Great Britain, the Church of England and the Roman Catholic Church. The REB set out to use 'clear and up-to-date but dignified language that will speak in a natural and understandable way to all'. In Paul's two letters to Timothy the revisers have cleared up some of those unfamiliar words, but they have kept: interminable, patricides, matricides, fidelity, implacable, insinuate and charlatans and have added, avaricious and perfidious. The English language is one of the richest in the world with one million words, but the revisers would have done well to appreciate that the average English speaker uses less than six thousand words—and those nine are probably not among them.

They also gave us 'pompous ignoramus' and, to a modern ear, the quaint eighteenth century phrase 'reformation of manners'. Sadly the word 'bishop' is retained at 1 Timothy 3:2; and 2 Timothy 3:16 kept, 'All inspired Scripture has its use...' which is not simply weak but wrong.

THE *NEW INTERNATIONAL VERSION*—A TRANSLATION

Since its completion in 1973, the *New International Version* (NIV) rapidly became the translation used by a significant number of evangelicals. Translated by an international team, mainly North American, of one hundred scholars who hold 'a high view of Scripture as set forth in the Westminster Confession of Faith, the Belgic Confession, and the Statement of Faith of the National Association of Evangelicals', the NIV could not fairly be accused of deliberately twisting Christian doctrine.

Based upon an eclectic text, it will never be accepted by those who favour the *Received Text* only. It can be criticized for its inconsistency in the footnotes that refer to 'other ancient authorities'. For example, at John 5:3–4 these disputed verses, which have some good manuscript backing, are relegated to the footnote with the comment that 'Some less important manuscripts' also add verse 4 (the 2011 revision changed this to 'Some manuscripts include here'), whereas at Acts 8:37, where the textual evidence of this verse is very sparse (even the *Received Text* omits it) we are simply informed that 'Some late manuscripts' add verse 37 (the 2011 revision has 'Some manuscripts include here'). The NIV is sometimes more likely to follow the *Septuagint* than the Masoretic text, as for example at Isaiah 53:11.

The second person singular ('thee' and 'thou') is omitted altogether, as are capital letters for pronouns relating to Deity ('his', 'him' etc); this is a wise move. Modern language has been used in a dignified way; for example, the mysterious 'jot and tittle' of Matthew 5:18 becomes 'not the smallest letter, not the least stroke of a pen'. There are many occasions of helpful translations making clear a hard passage, for example John 1:13 becomes: 'children born not of natural descent, nor of human decision or a husband's will, but born of God'.

Of course, there are inconsistencies and blemishes, but there are also some strikingly good translations. The 1984 NIV was an excellent translation for public reading because it used easy English and avoided some of the unnecessary repetitions of single words found in the Greek. The small conjunctions *kai* and *de* ('and' or 'but') are scattered liberally across the Greek text but do not always require translating. To take a chapter at random, Mark 14 begins a sentence forty times with the word *kai*, but the NIV translates it 'and' on only four occasions and more often correctly ignores it altogether. This makes for a much smoother reading and loses nothing of the meaning.

NEW INTERNATIONAL VERSION 2011—A REVISION

Two attempts at revision were carried out in 2002 and 2005 but the negative response to the extreme attempts at 'gender neutrality' in the text meant that they were both withdrawn. In 2011 these two failed versions were revised and published by Zondervan. The new attempt to grapple with the gender issue has already been discussed above under 'Translating gender'. For some, the broad attempt at gender neutrality has turned a good translation into a poor one. In addition to what was said earlier there are a host of other gender changes that are questionable. Some will consider this 'too high a price to pay for attaining gender-inclusiveness in a translation'.[94] One example will illustrate this: Psalm 8:4 'What is *mankind* that you are mindful of them, *human beings* that you care for them?' The Hebrew was correctly translated in 1984, 'What is man that you are mindful of him, the son of man that you care for him?' The NIV 2011 change is unnecessary and unfortunate since it loses entirely the connection with Hebrews 2:6 and the title 'Son of Man' in the Gospels. The *New Living Translation* (see below) makes the same mistake but at least adds a footnote in Psalm 8:4 to tell the reader what the Hebrew really says.

---

94 A report on-line (6 June 2011) from the Council on Biblical Manhood and Womanhood offers a full discussion on the errors of gender translation in the NIV 2011.

On more than fifteen hundred occasions the new NIV has changed the masculine singular (he, him, his) into a plural (they, them, their). This means that readers can no longer know whether the original text used a singular or plural masculine pronoun. Nor can they make a judgement in any particular text whether the use of 'men' as opposed to 'men and women' carried significance or not.

The significance of careful accuracy is illustrated in 1 Timothy 2:12, 'I do not permit a woman to *assume* authority over a man'. This allows the possibility that a woman can take authority if it is not 'assumed'. Whether that is a correct *interpretation* is not the translators task, but it is certainly not a correct *translation* of the word Paul used, which means 'to have authority' or 'to exercise authority'.

The avoidance of the word 'saints' (*hagioi*) is understandable, and 'God's holy people' might be considered a useful alternative as a translation of the Greek at, for example, Ephesians 1:1. However, merely to translate the same significant word as 'his people' in 4:12 is an unfortunate slip.

Overall, this is a good translation, although for many, these unwise attempts at gender neutrality may make the NIV 2011 unsuitable for either private or congregational study. The 1984 edition is no longer available.

THE *LIVING BIBLE*—A PARAPHRASE
Kenneth Taylor produced this paraphrase, completing the New Testament in 1962 and the Old Testament in 1971. The language, for its day, was racy, down to earth and at times coarse. A few examples will illustrate its attempt to be contemporary. Romans 9:21 is rendered, 'one jar beautiful, to be used for holding flowers, and another to throw garbage into'; and Romans 14:7: 'We are not our own bosses'; whilst in 1 Samuel 24:3 we have the plainly ridiculous statement that Saul 'went into a cave to go to the bathroom.'

There is too much of Taylor's interpretation in his paraphrase. For example, at Genesis 37:6,9 we read, '"Listen to this", he *proudly* announced...' and '"Listen to my latest dream" he *boasted*.' The words 'proudly' and 'boasted' appear nowhere in the Hebrew text; this may be what Taylor thought of Joseph—and he may be right—but nowhere does God's word say so.

More serious is Taylor's ability to obscure the true meaning of a verse. There can be no defence for such a weakness, since the only justification for a paraphrase is its ability to make the text clear. The following examples are a few of many:

> 'God treats everyone the same' (Romans 2:11). God does not. The word is 'partiality' (ESV) and Paul means that in God's dealings with man he is not influenced by circumstances or traditions.

> 'He used Christ's blood and our faith as the means of saving us from his wrath' (Romans 3:25). Our faith is not additional to the blood of Christ; it is faith *in* the blood of Christ that saves us.

> 'And we know that all that happens to us is working for our good if we love God and are fitting into his plans' (Romans 8:28). 'Fitting into his plans' is a strange way even to paraphrase 'called according to his purpose'.

The *Living Bible* was very popular, and certainly reads easily; however, accuracy is the more important requirement for any Bible translation or paraphrase.

THE *NEW LIVING TRANSLATION*—A TRANSLATION/PARAPHRASE

In 1996 a revision of the *Living Bible* came onto the Bible market as the *New Living Bible*. It was revised in 2004 and 2007. Although it is a revision of the *Living Bible*, it claims to be no longer a paraphrase but a translation based on the principle of 'dynamic equivalence'. The stated aim was to 'have the same impact on modern readers as the original had on its own audience', and to be 'exegetically accurate and idiomatically powerful.' Importantly, the translators recognised that the 'biblical documents were written to be read aloud, often in public worship'—a point that seems to be overlooked in some Bible translations. On this issue, the NLT fulfils its mission extremely well.

The NLT wisely moved away from Kenneth Taylor's interpretation of Joseph in Genesis 37:6,9 but unfortunately retained 'all Scripture is inspired by God' at 2 Timothy 3:16. However, Romans 3:25 becomes, 'God sent Jesus to take the punishment for our sins and to satisfy Gods anger against us' which, if we must lose 'propitiation', is a fair explanation of the word. The strong New Testament word 'grace' becomes 'God's special favour'.

At times it is colloquial to the point of reading far more into the original: Mark 14:72 vividly reads, 'Suddenly, Jesus' words flashed through Peter's mind', perhaps they did, but 'remembered' is quite sufficient. We may question whether 'the Roman coin used for the tax' (Matthew 22:19) is better than 'denarius' since this was the daily pay of a labourer and legionary, or whether the fact that the disciples were 'commercial fishermen' is necessary. But these are small criticisms of a translation that certainly reads well and makes good sense, especially in the prophetical books. Isaiah 9:7, 'The passionate commitment of the Lord Almighty will guarantee this' is an example.

It should be noted that the NLT follows the gender-neutral approach and 'brethren' generally becomes 'brothers and sisters'. The problems of this have been noted above with the *New International Version 2011*, although the NLT manages to avoid some of the pitfalls more neatly than the NIV. For public reading the *New Living Translation* is excellent, although because it is at times more of a paraphrase, and because of its gender-neutral policy, it may not be the most suitable study Bible.

THE *NEW KING JAMES VERSION*—A REVISION

In 1982 a revision of the *King James Version*, based solely upon the *Received Text*, was completed and published by Thomas Nelson as the *Revised Authorized Version*. The same revision, with a few spelling adjustments, is now known as the *New King James Version* (NKJV).

This is not a new translation but a revision, and therefore ideally suited to those who love the *King James Version*, or by conviction prefer the *Received Text* to any other, and yet who need a language update. This approach has at times limited the freedom of the revisers: for example, they have retained the old-fashioned and inaccurate 'inspiration' at 2 Timothy 3:16 instead of 'God-breathed', and 1 John 5:7 is retained in spite of the overwhelming textual evidence against it. However, in places the NKJV allows itself the freedom of improving on the *King James Version*, so that Paul's 'God forbid' becomes more correctly, 'Certainly not' and at Matthew 27:44, 'cast the same in his teeth' becomes simply 'reviled him with the same thing'. In 2 Peter 1:1 the NKJV follows other modern translations by making clear, as the Greek does, that Christ is both God and Saviour; this is an important improvement on the *King James Version*. So is the 'one flock' of John 10:16 instead of the 'one fold' in the *King James Version*.

The NKJV rejects the principle of 'dynamic equivalence', according to which a modern idiom is chosen in place of one reflecting Bible times; the translators opted for 'complete equivalence' instead; this may be seen as an improvement even on the *King James Version*. Generally the translators have fulfilled their commitment in the production of a carefully accurate translation of their Greek text.

The use of the second person singular to refer to Deity is dropped. But this wise decision seems to cut across the use of capital letters to refer to Christ throughout, which makes for a clumsy appearance with a liberal use of 'You', 'Him', 'He', 'Who', and even 'Man'. This is not just a matter of preference, because the system forces the translators to decide when and where the reference is to a person of the Godhead; this presents problems in the Old Testament prophetic references to Christ, and in the New Testament prior to the ascension of Christ. Even more debatable is the decision to place the words of Christ in red—a habit that serves little purpose and brings with it the danger of suggesting, though unintentionally, that the actual words of Christ are more important than the rest of Scripture—fortunately non-red-letter editions are available. The footnotes reveal references to alternative readings from the Nestle Greek Text, the 'NU-Text', which is not tied to the *Received Text*.

Often important shades of meaning are well captured, as for example, Peter's reference to 'your *own* husbands' in 1 Peter 3:1 where the word 'own' is too frequently overlooked by translators. Similarly Hebrews 1:3

where their Greek text is accurately rendered: 'when he had *by himself* purged our sins'. In Ephesians, Paul's frequent use of the little preposition 'with' as a prefix is captured by the often use of the word 'together'; clearly the translators realised what Paul was doing in his letter. It is also good to find a translation that appreciates that the word in Colossians 2:16 is best translated 'sabbaths' and not 'a Sabbath day'.

The NKJV is an accurate translation, though for public reading it still sounds archaic with such phrases as 'my beloved' ('my dear friend') and 'the fruit of your womb' ('the child you will bear'). At times the translation can be wooden (see for example Exodus 6:28–29); and such phrases as 'in like manner', 'did not heed them' and 'Thus … behold' (Exodus 7:11–13,17) do not help a modern reader.

In 2014 the *Modern English Version* published by Charisma House came onto the market. It is a new translation based upon the *Masoretic Text* (Old Testament) and the *Received Text* (New Testament) and is therefore in the same 'family' as the NKJV. Capital pronouns are reserved for deity.

THE *ENGLISH STANDARD VERSION*—A TRANSLATION/REVISION

In 2001 Crossways, a division of Good News Publishers in America, published the *English Standard Version* (ESV) with the stated goal of 'Faithfulness to the text and vigorous pursuit of accuracy … combined with simplicity, beauty, and dignity of expression.' To this end, every phrase was compared to the original Hebrew, Aramaic and Greek to ensure that nuances in the text were observed. The *Revised Standard Version* was 'the starting point for our work'. The ESV claims to be an 'essentially literal' translation which means that as far as possible it follows the line of 'formal equivalence' (literal translation) rather than 'functional equivalence' (paraphrase). It shows a marked preference for the *Masoretic Text* (against the *Septuagint* or Dead Sea texts) but by using the Nestle and Aland Greek text, the ESV is clearly eclectic in its choice, which will not be acceptable to those who favour the *Received Text*. The international team of scholars (heavily weighted towards North America) were committed to 'the truth of God's Word and to historic Christian orthodoxy'—this meant they held generally to biblical inerrancy. The text was lightly revised in 2007.

The ESV tends towards gender inclusiveness, for example using 'anyone' instead of 'any man', where this is possible—but not to the point of losing the word 'brothers' when this refers to all Christians. We may wonder whether 'people-pleasers', instead of man-pleasers in Ephesians 6:6, is necessary, especially as the word 'man' is retained in the next verse.

At times the 'nuances' are well understood when, for example, Peter urged wives to 'be subject to *your own* husbands' (1 Peter 3:1), a subtle point missed by many translations, and it well translates 2 Peter 1:9 as 'so nearsighted that he is blind'; similarly, the woman could not '*fully* straighten herself' in Luke 13:11—the most accurate way to translate *pantelés*.

Unfortunately, at 1 Corinthians 6:9 only one word is translated by 'men who practise homosexuality' whereas Paul used two words: *malakoi* (effeminate) and *arsenokoitai* (sodomy); it would certainly assist in today's debate if both words had been translated. By ignoring the *Received Text* in Hebrews 1:3 the ESV loses the significance of a single word captured by the NKJV 'When he had *by himself* purged our sins…'

Some translations are surprising: is 'vanity' really the best word in Ecclesiastes 1:2 etc? *The Oxford English Dictionary* defines it as 'conceit' and 'a desire for personal admiration'—which is not what the Hebrew intends. Many phrases are hardly modern: 'unto you' (Luke 2:11); 'That it be not known', 'his eyes were dim', 'Thus and thus you shall say', (1 Kings 14:1–5); 'seeking to see' and 'small of stature' (Luke 19:3); 'kill them not' (Psalm 59:11); 'a womb or two for each man' (Judges 5:30), 'on the pate of him who … (Deuteronomy 33:16), and 'unto you' (Luke 2:11) are just a few. The frequent use of 'Behold' could be improved. The North American editors would have been wise to consult from the other side of the Atlantic before allowing, for example: 'When I have *gotten* glory over Pharaoh' (Exodus 14:16) and 'those who hate us have *gotten* spoil' (Psalm 44:10); admittedly this is *King James Version* language but it grates on a modern British congregation.

The ESV does not always read well publicly. 1 Kings 14:7–10 is rendered as one sentence of one hundred and fifty words, where the *New*

International Version (2011) helpfully gave us six sentences. Then, 'the earth brings forth its sprouts' (Isaiah 61:11) will amuse even the least of the gourmets in the congregation; why not 'shoots', 'buds' or 'young plants'?

It is hardly imaginative translation to begin fifty-three sentences with 'and' in Mark 14 where even the Greek *kai* occurs only forty times to open a sentence. (The NIV reduced this to four.) Together with the fifty-seven uses in mid-verse 'and' is repeated one hundred and seven times in seventy-two verses—the same number as in the Greek. The ESV frequently, and unnecessarily, binds itself to translate this small conjunction which makes less than smooth public reading.

Some of the above are relatively small criticisms of what is a faithful translation and generally to be commended for its accuracy and theological loyalty. Although the ESV may not be the best for public reading, the over-zealous gender-neutrality of the NIV 2011 and the NLT may mean that for evangelicals looking for an accurate, fairly contemporary, translation not restricted to the *Received Text*, the ESV will perhaps be their obvious choice. It is a reliable study Bible.

THE *CHRISTIAN STANDARD BIBLE*—A TRANSLATION

This recent translation began life in 2004 as the *Holman Christian Standard Bible* and was revised by one hundred scholars from seventeen denominations, largely North American. In 2017, 'Holman' was dropped from the title. Whilst using an eclectic text, the translators adopted an 'optimal equivalence' approach which they claim is somewhere between 'formal equivalence' (word for word) and 'dynamic equivalence (thought for thought, or, meaning for meaning). It is claimed that the CSB is more literal than the NIV and more readable than the ESV.

As would be expected, some renderings are excellent, but at times a translation decision may seem odd. The consistent change from 'O God' in the psalms is strange to those who value the vocative; thus, for example, 'God, how precious your thoughts are to me; how vast their sum is!' (Psalm 139:17) is wooden and quite hard to read publicly with the intensity of 'How precious to me are your thoughts, O God! How vast is the sum of them!'

The revisers followed the gender-neutral approach systematically and therefore face the criticisms that can be made against other similar translations. For example, in 2 Timothy 2:2 Paul encouraged Timothy to entrust the Christian message to 'reliable men' who 'will be qualified to teach others'; by translating the masculine plural with 'people' the translators are assuming that Paul was allowing the women to teach in the church, something he explicitly forbade in 1 Timothy 2:12.

In Romans 3:25, the translators opted for the far weaker 'atoning sacrifice' in place of 'propitiation'; a common fault of many modern translations. Surprisingly, and against all current understanding of the word, CSB has chosen to retain 'inspired' in 2 Timothy 3:16 instead of 'God-breathed'. At times the reader would prefer a more colloquial, and equally accurate rendering—at Mark 14:19 'surely not me?' would be better than 'surely not I?'

As with the NIV revision some reviewers express a preference for the earlier translation rather than the new revision. For those who are comfortable with a gender-neutral translation, the CSB will stand alongside the *New International Version* (2011) and the *New Living Translation* as a useful translation since it reads well publicly.

The next two Bible versions can best be summarized by the way they each begin and close their translations. Here is Genesis 1:1–2 and Revelation 22:21 first in *The Message* and then, for comparison, in *The Word on the Street*:

The Message: 'First this: God created the Heaven and the Earth—all you see, all you don't see. Earth was a soup of nothingness, a bottomless emptiness, an inky blackness. God's Spirit brooded like a bird above the watery abyss.'

Then to close the Bible: 'The grace of the Master Jesus be with all of you. Oh, Yes!'

The Word on the Street: 'First off, nothing ... but God. No light, no time, no substance, no matter. Second off, God says the word and WHAP! Stuff everywhere! The cosmos in chaos: no shape, no form, no function—just darkness … total. And floating above it all, God's Holy Spirit, ready to play.'

Then to close the Bible: '"Here's to Jesus the Boss pouring out his generosity on God's people. Absolutely!'

These comparisons clearly show the shift in dynamic presentation in the short space from 2002 to 2003!

THE MESSAGE—A VERY LOOSE PARAPHRASE

The Message is published by NavPress, presented by Eugene Peterson and subtitled 'The Bible in contemporary language'. Jim Packer, Peterson's fellow Professor at Regent College in Vancouver, commends it as a 'blend of accurate scholarship and vivid idiom.' Chapter divisions are kept, but to make it read more like a book, verses are excluded; as Peterson correctly points out, there were no verses in our Bible for fifteen hundred years. Each book of the Bible begins with a short introductory section and the flow of the text is undoubtedly attractive. It is contemporary without being crass, and it certainly uses the language of today. Provided that we are not looking for the nuances that a straight translation should have, there is something to commend *The Message* to a non-church and lightly-educated reader.

Peterson set out to prepare a text that people who had no interest in the Bible would be attracted to, without dumbing down the message; he urges the readers to move on and get 'a standard study Bible' as soon as possible. It can only be hoped that all readers take his advice because that standard study Bible will certainly be needed: whilst Peterson is good at reporting narrative, he fails sadly when the heart of the Gospel is at stake. The phrase in Romans 3:25, 'Whom God put forward as a propitiation by his blood, to be received by faith' (ESV) turns into: 'God sacrificed Jesus on the altar of the world to clear that world of sin. Having faith in him sets us in the clear.' Certainly 'propitiation' is a hard word to modernize, but what does 'the altar of the world' mean?

There are some renderings that are faithful to the heart of the meaning and read with life and enthusiasm. As an example, 2 Timothy 3:14–17 will provide a fair opportunity to assess its merits:

'But don't let it faze you. Stick with what you learned and believed, sure of the integrity of your teachers—why, you took in the sacred Scriptures with your mother's milk! There's nothing like the written Word of God for showing you the way to salvation through faith in Christ Jesus. Every part of Scripture is God-breathed and useful one way or another—showing us truth, exposing our rebellion, correcting our mistakes, training us to live God's way. Through the Word we are put together and shaped up for the tasks God has for us.'

Similarly, the end of Romans 8 reads well: 'I'm absolutely convinced that nothing—nothing living or dead, angelic or demonic, today or tomorrow, high or low, thinkable or unthinkable—absolutely *nothing* can get between us and God's love because of the way that Jesus our Master has embraced us.'

However, inevitably a paraphrase like this loses much of the strength and precision of the Scriptures. As a way *in* for someone who may be tempted to read the Bible if it is in a more familiar style, *The Message* may prove useful, but certainly it is of little value for the *way on*, and it has no place in the serious public reading of Scripture, or for personal study purposes. *The Message* is an entertaining read, but as with all paraphrases, accuracy is sacrificed for readability.

THE WORD ON THE STREET—A VERY LOOSE PARAPHRASE

Rob Lacey has taken the entertainment one step further, and perhaps to its conclusion. Originally *The Street Bible*, it was first published in 2003 and a year later was voted Christian Book of the Year in the UK. *The Word on the Street* is 'For those who've never read the Bible, and for those who've read it too much.' To be fair, it does not claim to be the Bible at all, and the hard bits, like Leviticus are dismissed in one paragraph of racy explanation—'messing up God's order makes him mad'—and Numbers with little more. It is hard to find your way around the Gospels, since they are compressed into one story with references to show where we are. But what can *The Word on the Street* make of the 'propitiation 'passage that *The Message* missed so badly? Interestingly it gets much closer to the meaning. This passage from Romans 3:23–26 will give a fair view of the style of *The Word on the Street*:

'No one's innocent. We've all messed up and dropped well short of God's target for us. But at no cost to us, he sets us straight and sorted, 'cos he bought us back with the priceless currency of Jesus' blood when he was ceremoniously sacrificed. And, no, God's not just wangled it; he's not pulled a fast one, or gone soft on us just to get us off the hook—it's all totally above board. See, Jesus took the rap that we should've got. So God stuck to the Rules, and still got us out of our mess, for those who take Jesus at his word.'

Isaiah 53 and the suffering of Christ is handled like this:

'He grew up vulnerable as a sapling in a concrete yard … He was dissed by most, given the cold shoulder by many … But whoa! Step back a sec! Weren't those our weaknesses he took on? Wasn't that our sadness he carried? … He was messed up for our mess. He was knocked down for our slip-ups. The slapping that we should've got—he got.'

There are some interesting ways of handling theological words such as:

'So they swivel round a full 180 degrees and face the music' (Zechariah 1:6b)—repentance.

'If we face up to it, admit to God that we've messed up' (1 John 1:9)—confession.

Much of the poetry is upgraded for the twenty-first century such as the Song of Solomon: 'Your voice carries your ideas like a chauffeur-driven Merc purring out from between your two crafted cheekbones…'.

Lacey communicates brilliantly, and for some, and only some, the language is right on! Although unlike Tyndale's concern for his ploughboy, Lacey is more concerned for entertainment than precision. But if we believe in verbal inspiration, precision matters above all. There is nothing intentionally coarse about *The Word on the Street*. Whatever our reaction to it, it is not mocking Scripture but taking it seriously.

However much we may enjoy settling down to a comfortable and entertaining read of *The Message* or *The Word on the Street*, these contemporary and light-weight paraphrases will never help us to grasp the great truths that God is revealing through a careful translation. If they introduce the non-churched and non-reader to the Bible, little harm may be done; but unless readers are quickly weaned to an accurate translation they will never grow in faith and understanding. We need a translation we can *trust* as well as enjoy.

With good reason, some may well consider that from the fifth century to the twenty-first, as far as translations are concerned, we have in some cases moved from the *Vulgate* to the vulgar.

CONCLUSION

Faced with a bewildering selection of translations, paraphrases and revisions, the average Christian is ill-equipped to make an informed judgement between them. Generally, Christians use the one their church or spiritual adviser recommends, or the one they grew up with. But there are an increasing number today who grew up with nothing. Some simply follow the trend by purchasing the one that sells best (popularity), others decide according to the quality of the cover or art-work inside (presentation), whilst others go for the modern language used (punchy), and some are merely influenced by a cheap edition (price). The choice of translations creates confusion especially among new readers of the Bible, and it makes it almost impossible for some congregations to read together aloud in worship. In some places, the choice of translation or paraphrase becomes a test of orthodoxy—and therefore of fellowship.

No translation will be perfect and satisfy everyone, and it is easy to criticise a few poorly rendered verses. Our decision needs to be based on whether these are widely typical or not.

There are a few areas that will focus the choice of a translation. The choice may depend on our preference for one family of Greek texts over others—the *Received Text* or an eclectic text. We may also want to be assured that it is essentially a translation rather than a loose paraphrase. For public reading, we will need to consider whether it reads easily and in contemporary language without losing the cultural context of the original setting. Similarly, a decision has to be made on the principle of gender-neutral words and phrases and whether or not a particular translation goes too far.

If all this is confusing, remember that the reactionary clerics of Wycliffe's and Tyndale's day feared the confusion caused by English translations! However, surely this is a price worth paying for the privilege of everyone across the English-speaking world being able to read God's word in their mother tongue. It is true that Tyndale worked hard to produce a Bible that would be understood by ordinary people—unlike the Latin of Jerome that was unintelligible to most—but Tyndale was equally meticulous to be accurate and faithful to the original Hebrew and Greek. He was a superb translator, and he knew the importance of a Bible that was in reality the word of God.

Index to significant subjects

These references will take the reader only to the book and chapter (eg 1/3, 4/5) in this series where the more significant references to the subject occur.

Index to significant subjects

Index to significant subjects

Index to significant subjects

Index to main Scripture references

These references will take the reader only to the book and chapter (eg 1/3, 4/5) in this series where the more significant Scripture references occur.

EVIDENCE
for the BIBLE

Clive Anderson and
Brian Edwards

LARGE FORMAT HARDBACK
FULL COLOUR THROUGHOUT
225mm × 275mm
260pp | ISBN 978-1-84625-416-1
REF EFB4161 | £25.00

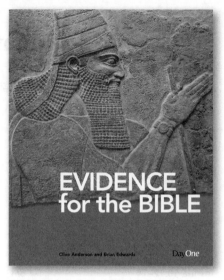

Evidence will surprise and inform you as you turn over the soil of history with the pages of your Bible. The witness of the trowel authenticates and illuminates the people and events, lifting them from the pages of the Book and setting them in the context of time and place. Join us on an exciting journey with this evidence from the past.

Evidence for the Bible can be found in many places, from the Ancient Near East to museums and private collections. Whilst artefacts can never prove the authority of the Bible, they can and do show that the events described in the Bible occurred in time and history.

This book provides a selection of the many items that demonstrate the reliability of the Bible as a historical document.

'Clive Anderson and Brian Edwards have captured the essence of generations of middle-eastern archaeology, historical context and biblical landscape in a quite remarkable way. Their book is accessible, informative and enjoyable. The pictures beautifully complement the text. The Bible comes alive. I warmly and wholeheartedly commend it to everyone who wishes to be a little wiser and better informed about the Book which has formed our culture and is the source of the Christian Faith.'
THE VERY REVD JAMES ATWELL,
Dean of Winchester.

'This is a marvellous introduction to the finds of archaeology that illumine our understanding of the Bible. It helps the reader to see that the biblical events and writings took place within history. When the reader studies the Bible, this book will serve as a wonderful tool to help get at its depth and richness. I highly recommend it.'
DR JOHN D CURRID
Carl McMurray Professor of Old Testament at the Reformed Theological Seminary, Charlotte, USA.

Through the British Museum with the Bible

Clive Anderson and Brian Edwards

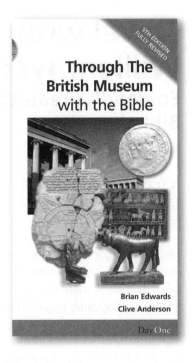

FULL COLOUR TRAVEL GUIDE
128pp | ISBN 978-1-90308-754-6
REF TWBM | £10.00

This guide centres on those items in the British Museum that are related to the history recorded in the Bible. You will be introduced to rulers, empires and cultures that, without the careful work of many scholars, would have been lost for ever. In this guide you have all that you need to make your tour both enjoyable and relevant. The past is brought to light in front of you.

'The British Museum is a great storehouse of treasures from the past; the Bible is the greatest treasure of all. This guide brings them together in a concise way that will help readers to understand more clearly what each has to offer.'

—ALAN MILLARD, *Rankin Professor Emeritus of Hebrew and Ancient Semitic Languages, The University of Liverpool. Formerly Assistant Keeper of Western Asiatic Antiquities at the British Museum.*

'I am delighted that this fine guide is available in a second and fully revised edition. The British Museum is unique worldwide for its collection of antiquities which illustrate Bible times and customs and this guide enables anyone, either alone or with a group, to identify them accurately. It is both reliable and easy to use.'

—DONALD J. WISEMAN, *Professor Emeritus of Assyriology in the University of London, formerly Assistant Keeper in the Egyptian and Western Asiatic Antiquities at the British Museum and President of the British School of Archaeology in Iraq.*

Travel with William Tyndale

England's greatest Bible translator

Brian H Edwards

FULL COLOUR TRAVEL GUIDE
128pp | ISBN 978-1-84625-160-3
REF TWWT1603 | £10.00

Melvyn Bragg in 'The Adventure of English' claims that William Tyndale wrote 'the most influential book there has ever been in the history of language, English or any other.' That is not too extravagant to describe the significance of Tyndale's translation into English of the whole of the New Testament and much of the Old from the original Greek and Hebrew. Tyndale is undoubtedly one of the greatest Englishmen ever, and all who speak this language owe him a great debt.

'This is a guide not only to Tyndale's places in England and on the continent, but also to his time, his ideas and his spirit. It is based on meticulous research and profound scholarly insight, whilst remaining very readable and entertaining.'
GUIDO LATRÉ, *University of Louvain*

Additional commendations

'This superb series provides a set of quality tools, enabling every thoughtful Christian to know how to answer the Bible's critics and grow in their own confidence and appreciation of God's living and enduring Word. Packed with valuable factual information, detailed documentation, wide-ranging references and penetrating reasoning, not a sceptical stone is left unturned and not a critical argument goes unanswered.

Here is a comprehensive and greatly needed resource, which deserves to be required reading for every believer as we seek to live by God's inerrant revelation and present its message with authenticity to an unbelieving world. I could not commend the series more warmly.'

DAVID JACKMAN, *author, former President of the Proclamation Trust and founder of the Cornhill Training Course*

'A superb collection, readable and reliable, with lots of footnotes to check out the material presented. A terrific resource for both believers and those seeking faith. Students at Moorlands will love this series. Highly recommended!'

DR STEVE BRADY, *Principal, Moorlands College, Christchurch*

'*All you need to know about the Bible* blends apologetics, history and biblical studies to produce this important and hugely enjoyable series. It provides the reader with a mental landscape within which a confident and intelligent love for the Bible can be nurtured. It is a tour de force and a marvellous gift to the church in our secular age. I could not commend it more warmly or enthusiastically.'

RICHARD CUNNINGHAM, *Director, Universities and Colleges Christian Unions*

'Accessible throughout, these comprehensive introductory accounts of Scripture will be of immense value to everyone who reads them. They go far beyond a simple introduction and probe deeply into the nature of the Bible as the faultless Word of God, considering and answering a full range of criticisms. Moreover, Brian writes in a manner that will benefit the newest Christian. I hope his work receives the widest possible readership.'

DR ROBERT LETHAM, *Professor of Systematic and Historical Theology, Union School of Theology, Wales*

Additional commendations

'This series of attractive, accessible introductions offers a feast of wisdom and insight into the origins and accuracy of the Bible. When navigating the complex issues surrounding ancient texts and modern translations, here is an excellent place to begin—a helpful guide to the basics of history, archaeology and manuscript evidence. Most importantly, the series encourages us to delight afresh in the truthfulness, sufficiency and authority of God's Word. These volumes will be of assistance to every Bible student.'

DR ANDREW ATHERSTONE, *Latimer Research Fellow, Wycliffe Hall, Oxford*

'The overwhelming strength of Brian's comprehensive series is that it provides ordinary Christians with confidence in the authority of the Bible. Brian has the skill to make this subject accessible without simplification or omission. What a great resource for Christians, equipping us to be on the front foot when it comes to defending the Bible against its many detractors!'

ADRIAN REYNOLDS,
author, local church pastor and Training Director of the Fellowship of Independent Evangelical Churches

'Each one of these books is a valuable guide to the teaching and historical reliability of the Bible. Together, the set builds a compelling case for the authority of Scripture as the very words of God with life-changing power. A wealth of material in readable style, it is a rich resource, giving fresh confidence in the reliability and authority of the Scriptures.'

BILL JAMES,
Principal, The London Seminary

'Like a jeweller turning a diamond so that every facet flashes with light, Brian holds up God's Word so that its perfections shine. Although my views differ from his on Bible translations, these books serve well to answer helpfully numerous objections, confirm faith, and wisely guide in profitable reading of the Word.'

DR JOEL R. BEEKE,
President, Puritan Reformed Theological Seminary, Grand Rapids, Michigan